THE POCKET fat, carbohydrate & fiber counter

Carol Bateman

BARNES & NOBLE BOOKS
NEW YORK

This edition published by Barnes & Noble Inc.,
by arrangement with Parragon Publishing

2004 Barnes & Noble Books

M 10 9 8 7 6 5 4 3 2 1

ISBN 0-7607-5526-4

Copyright © 2004 by Parragon

Printed and bound in Indonesia

Nutrition Consultants: Stephanie Green RD, and Fiona Hunter

Photographer: Karen Thomas

Home Economist: Valerie Berry

Illustrations: Anna Hunter-Downing

NOTES

 This symbol means the recipe is suitable for vegetarians.

This book uses imperial, metric, or US cup measurements. Follow the same units of measurement throughout; do not mix imperial and metric.

All spoon measurements are level: teaspoons are assumed to be 5 ml, and tablespoons are assumed to be 15 ml. Unless otherwise stated, eggs and individual vegetables such as potatoes are assumed to be medium, and pepper is freshly ground black pepper.

Recipes using raw or very lightly cooked eggs should be avoided by infants, the elderly, pregnant women, convalescents, and anyone suffering from an illness. Pregnant and breastfeeding women are advised to avoid eating peanuts and peanut products.

The times given are an approximate guide only. Preparation times differ according to the techniques used by different people and the cooking times may also vary from those given. Optional ingredients, variations, or serving suggestions have not been included in the calculations.

Before you follow any advice given in this book, we recommend that you first check with your physician. Pregnant women, women planning to become pregnant, children, diabetics, or people with other medical conditions should always check with their physician or health care professional before embarking on any type of diet. This book is not intended as a substitute for your physician's or dietician's advice and support, but should complement the advice they give you. The accuracy of the nutritional information (calorie, fat, and salt) given for each recipe is dependent on following the recipe instructions

CONTENTS

Why a Fat, Carbohydrate & Fiber Counter?   4

The Food Pyramid   6

Using the Counter   8

Energy & Body Weight   10

Food Labeling   11

Foods A–Z Counter   12

The Glycemic Index (GI)   94

Essential Vitamins & Minerals   96

Healthy Recipes for You   97

WHY A FAT, CARBOHYDRATE, AND FIBER COUNTER?

Because balancing the amounts of fat, carbohydrate, and fiber we consume daily is vital to good health.

Your diet should provide all the energy, protein, vitamins, and minerals you need to stay healthy and active every day, allowing you to enjoy life to the fullest. In our affluent Western society, however, it is all too easy to consume a diet that is high in fat, sugar, and salt, and too low in fiber and nutrients. Our busy lifestyles often mean that we eat fast-food or ready-prepared foods. High-fat, high-sugar, high-salt diets may be harmful to your health, leading to increased risk of coronary heart disease, high blood pressure, and certain forms of cancer. Choosing to eat nutritious foods is important in achieving good health. Although there are no "good" or "bad" foods, the key to better health is selecting a variety of nutritious foods every day, and reducing the number of "empty" calorie foods that provide little in the way of nutrients.

The Pocket Fat, Carbohydrate & Fiber Counter is designed to help you achieve optimum health. It will help you understand the composition of a

wide range of foods and enable you to select and reach the daily nutritional requirements for you and your family.

The three energy nutrients that provide dietary calories are fat, carbohydrate, and protein. The number of calories you need depends on many factors, including your sex, weight, age, and activity level. The majority of the energy required should come from protein, fat, and carbohydrates.

While protein is essential for the growth and maintenance of body tissues, most adults eat more than enough. High-fiber foods also provide a significant amount of protein so by achieving your daily fiber goal, you can reach your protein needs.

The A–Z food listing focuses on counting three essential nutrition elements in the foods you choose: fat, carbohydrate, and fiber. (Although fiber is not a nutrient, it plays a vital role in good health.) If you follow the recommendations for daily intake of these nutrition elements, you will also obtain the vitamins and minerals essential for good health.

Aim to limit the fats and choose complex carbohydrates as opposed to simple (low-fiber) carbohydrates. Creating a healthy diet requires flexibility in food choices. For example, balance a higher fat and calorie day with a low fat/higher fiber meal the next day. Overall, try to achieve a healthy diet every day.

THE FOOD PYRAMID

This diagram shows the recommended balance of the five different food groups in your daily diet. The largest group is carbohydrates, followed by fruits and vegetables. Protein and dairy foods are next, with the smallest group containing the fats and sugars. Around half the total calories you need should come from complex carbohydrates and 30 percent from fats.

Foods containing fat, and foods containing sugar
Eat only small amounts each day

Milk and dairy foods
Eat 2–3 servings a day

Meat, fish, and alternatives
Eat 2–3 servings a day

Fruit and vegetables (high in fiber, low in calories)
Eat 5 servings a day

Carbohydrates
Eat 6–11 servings a day

Bread, other cereals, and potatoes

This group includes all foods such as bread, rolls, breakfast cereals, oats, pasta, noodles, rice, and cornmeal. Most of these foods are good sources of dietary fiber and contain other important nutrients. For good health, your goal should be to have 45–65 percent of your daily energy (calories) from this food group.

Fruits and vegetables

This includes all fresh, frozen, and canned fruits and vegetables, as well as beans, lentils, dried fruit and fruit juices. Try to choose a wide variety of fruits and vegetables—at least five servings every day—to get the important vitamins, minerals, and antioxidants they provide.

Milk and dairy foods

The dairy foods (milk, cheese, and yogurt) are all good sources of protein and minerals, especially calcium. Low-fat dairy products retain the calcium content of full-fat kinds. If avoiding dairy products, choose alternatives fortified with calcium.

Meat, fish, and meat alternatives

This group includes meats, such as beef, pork, bacon, lamb, and meat products (e.g. sausages, hotdogs); also poultry, fish, fish products, organ meats such as liver, eggs, beans and lentils, nuts and nut products, textured vegetable protein, and other meat alternatives. Protein should account for about 15 percent of one's total daily calories.

Fats, oils, and sugars

This includes butter, margarine, low-fat spreads, cooking oils, mayonnaise and oily salad dressings, cookies, cakes, puddings/desserts, ice cream, chocolate, candy, refined sugar, and sweetened drinks. Try to limit your intake of fatty and sugary foods.

USING THE COUNTER

The A–Z food counter lists the carbohydrate, fiber, and fat content per average serving. Everyone's fat and carbohydrate requirements differ slightly depending on their individual daily energy (calorie) needs. A normal-weight female aged 19–50 needs around 2,400 calories per day, while a normal-weight male of 19–50 needs around 3,000 calories. Follow these guides or estimate your own daily calorie needs using the calculation on page 10.

FAT

All fats contain a mixture of fatty acids: saturated, monounsaturated and polyunsaturated. While the kind of fat we eat can make a difference in our health, all types are equally high in calories. Fat in food may be visible (e.g. butter, oil) or invisible (e.g. cheese, meat).

Dietary fat raises total cholesterol in the bloodstream. High blood cholesterol increases the risk of coronary heart disease and other medical conditions. It is advisable to limit the total daily fat intake to no more than 30 percent of the total calories from fat, with no more than 10 percent from saturated fats.

Saturated fats are believed to raise the level of the harmful LDL (low density lipoprotein) cholesterol associated with heart disease. The omega-3 fatty acids (found in oily fish) may help to prevent clotting and reduce the risk of heart disease. Monounsaturated fats raise the ratio of beneficial HDL to LDL cholesterol and may also have a protective role in the prevention of coronary heart disease.

COUNTING FAT

A woman who needs 2,400 calories a day requires up to 30 percent (720 calories) to come from fats.

If 1 gram fat = 9 calories, the desired fat intake would be 80 g/day. A man using 3,000 calories needs no more than 100 g fat.

CARBOHYDRATE

The two types of carbohydrates are simple and complex. Simple carbohydrates are one- or two-molecule sugars like table sugar, composed of glucose and fructose. A complex carbohydrate contains hundreds of molecules linked together. Staple carbohydrates worldwide (bread, rice, potatoes, pasta, cassava, yam, plantains, and green bananas) are starchy carbohydrates. High-protein beans, lentils, seeds, and nuts also contain complex carbohydrates. Natural sugars are present in milk and many plant foods, especially fruit. Natural or refined sugars, occurring in honey and cane/beet sugars, are high in calories but provide little in the way of nutritional value.

COUNTING CARBOHYDRATES

A recommended 45–65 percent of daily energy (calories) should come from carbohydrates, the least amount coming from simple sugars. At a rate of 1 g carbohydrates = 4 calories, this works out to be 270–390 g carbohydrate (based on 2,400 calories) or 338–488 g (based on 3,000 calories) daily.

FIBER

This is the fibrous part of plant foods (cereals, fruit, vegetables, beans, nuts, seeds) that remains in the intestine after digestion. As humans, we can't digest fiber so it acts as nature's broom, keeping things moving through our system. This helps prevent constipation, coronary heart disease, gall bladder disease, and some cancers.

The recommended intake of dietary fiber is 25–30 g/day. To achieve this, eat plenty of wholegrain breads and cereals, as well as five servings of fruits and vegetables each day.

ENERGY & BODY WEIGHT

Are you the right weight for your height? To find out your body mass index (BMI) divide your weight in pounds by your height in inches squared:

30+	Obese—at increased risk of disease
26–29	Overweight—losing weight is recommended
19–25	Normal—within the healthy range
– 19	Underweight—need to gain weight

How much food energy you need each day varies according to your sex, age, weight, and activity level. The following equations will give an estimate of your energy requirements, but remember, these are very general calculations.

1. Use the equation for your sex and age, and add in your weight in pounds:

MEN

Age: 18–29: [(0.063 x weight) + 2.896] x 239

Age: 30–60: [(0.048 x weight) + 3.653] x 239

Age: Over 60: [(0.049 x weight) + 2.459] x 239

WOMEN

Age: 19–29: [(0.062 x weight) + 2.036] x 239

Age: 30–60: [(0.034 x weight) + 3.538] x 239

Age: Over 60: [(0.038 x weight) + 2.755] x 239

2. Although this gives you the basic calories you require, it does not include activity, so multiply the answer to equation 1 by your activity level.

First select the activity level for your job. A desk job will be "light," but a more active job such as nursing will be at least "moderate." If you exercise regularly, you will be moderately active but if you exercise rarely, your leisure activity level will be "light."

ADULTS	Occupational activity		
Leisure activity	Light	Moderate	Mod/ Heavy
	M F	M F	M F
Non-active	1.4 1.4	1.6 1.5	1.7 1.5
Moderately active	1.5 1.5	1.7 1.6	1.8 1.6
Very active	1.6 1.6	1.8 1.7	1.9 1.7

For an adult to lose weight, subtract about 500 calories from the daily requirement and use the counter to check food intake. Very low-calorie diets (below 1,200) are not a good way to lose weight. By making this smaller adjustment you will lose weight more gradually, and have a better chance of long-term success.

Note: Before starting any diet, check with your physician.

the pocket fat, carbohydrate & fiber counter

FOOD LABELING

Food labels provide information on the contents of cans, packages, and wrappings. The contents are listed in order of the percentage of each ingredient, with the largest quantity appearing first. Use this listing to compare similar products for content and value.

Nutrition labeling is required by the government to help the consumer make informed choices. Many products contain more than one serving in a package or can so it's important to learn how to read the nutrition facts panel.

The basic nutritional information found on a nutrition facts panel can be seen in the box (right).

When you go shopping for food use the label on cans, packages and wrapping to help select foods that are high in dietary fiber and low in sugar and to help you have a balanced diet.

Fats are shown as total fats, trans fats, and saturated fats. This information is helpful because any fat that is not saturated or trans will be mono- or polyunsaturated. This additional information may be

Nutritional Information Facts Panel

Serving size (as cups, g)
Servings per container (per person)
Calories (value)
Total fat (g and %)
  Saturated fat (g and %)
  Trans fats (g and %)
Cholesterol (mg and %)
Sodium (g and %)
Total carbohydrates (g and %)
  Dietary fiber (g and %)
  Sugar (g and %)
Protein (g and %)
Vitamin A (%)
Vitamin C (%)
Calcium (%)
Iron (%)

Percentage (%) of daily value, based on a 2000-calorie diet.

listed on the label. Labeling trans fatty acids is a new requirement for food manufacturers and the amount of trans fat is now included as part of the nutrition facts panel.

A

ALCOHOL

For many of us drinking alcohol is an enjoyable social activity. A glass of wine with a meal or a drink with friends is a pleasant way to relax at the end of the day.

Nutritional content

Alcohol is made from the yeast fermentation of different fruits or grains including grapes, hops, apples, and barley. Spirits are distilled and contain no sugar, while beers and wines have varying amounts. Alcoholic beverages contain almost no other nutritional value other than calories.

Medical benefits

In small amounts, alcoholic beverages such as red wine consumed on a regular basis may protect against some medical conditions including coronary heart disease. However, too much alcohol may cause weight gain and be harmful to health.

Moderation

It is wise to keep your intake of alcohol to sensible levels. One way is to check how many drinks you consume on a regular basis. A single serving of alcohol equals:

    12 fl oz beer
    5 fl oz wine
    1½ fl oz 80-proof distilled spirits

Moderation would encourage no more than two drinks per day for men and no more than one drink per day for women. Calories add up quickly and serving sizes vary. A typical glass of wine may be from 4–6 oz.

A

FOOD	FAT g	FIBER g	CARB g	ENERGY calories
ALCOHOL				
BEER				
lager, 12 fl oz	0	1	6	107
light beer, 12 fl oz	0	0	5	99
malt, 12 fl oz	0	0	12	167
pale ale, 12 fl oz	0	0	17	179
regular, 12 fl oz	0	1	13	146
stout, 12 fl oz	0	0	13	157
LIQUEURS				
higher strength,				
(Curaçao, Drambuie), 1 1/2 fl oz	0	0	19	150
lower strength,				
(cherry brandy, coffee) 1 1/2 fl oz	0	0	14	108
SPIRITS				
bourbon 80 proof, 1 1/2 fl oz	0	0	0	96
gin 80 proof, 1 1/2 fl oz	0	0	0	96
rum 80 proof, 1 1/2 fl oz	0	0	0	96
tequila, 80 proof, 1 1/2 fl oz	0	0	0	96
vodka 80 proof, 1 1/2 fl oz	0	0	0	98
WINES				
champagne, dry, 6 fl oz	0	0	6	126
port, 3 1/2 fl oz	0	0	12	158
red, dry, 6 fl oz	0	0	2	126
rosé, 6 fl oz	0	0	3	122
sherry, dry, 4 fl oz	0	0	4	250
sweet dessert, 4 fl oz	0	0	14	90
vermouth, dry, 1 fl oz	0	0	0	30

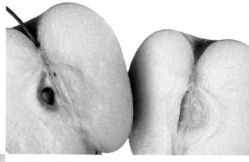

A

APPLES

Apples are a delicious and versatile food that can be used in many ways. They can be eaten raw as a crunchy snack, cooked and made into a sauce, baked by themselves or in pies or cakes.

A healthy snack

For most children apples are a favorite fruit. So when children ask for a snack, give them an apple instead of cookies or candy, and remember that an apple makes a crispy addition to a school lunch bag.

A healthy dessert

Enjoying a piece of naturally sweet fruit is a great way of ending a meal.

Nutritional content

Apples are a good source of fiber (about 4 g/apple) When an apple is peeled, about half the fiber is lost. One apple contains about 21 g carbohydrate.

FOOD	FAT	FIBER	CARB	ENERGY
	g	g	g	calories
(ALCOHOL)				
vermouth, sweet, 1 fl oz	0	0	4	46
white, medium, 6 fl oz	0	0	1	120
white, sparkling, sweet, 6 fl oz	0	0	12	138
wine cooler, 12 fl oz	0	0	20	170
COCKTAILS				
bloody mary, 5 fl oz	0	0	5	116
margarita cocktail, 8 fl oz	0	0	32	500
martini, dry, $2^1/_2$ fl oz	0	0	0	158
screwdriver cocktail, 8 fl oz	0	0	20	194
APPLE				
raw, unpeeled, 1 each	0.5	4	21	81
baked, unsweetened, 1 each	1	5	26	102
raw, peeled, 1 each	0.5	2.5	19	73
dried, $1/_4$ cup	2	0	14	52
juice, $3/_4$ cup	0	0	10	68
APRICOT				
canned in juice, $1/_2$ cup	2	0	15	59
canned in syrup, 4 halves	0	1	15	56
dried, 10 halves	0.5	8	15	66
raw, 3, each	0	2.5	9	37
ARTICHOKE				
globe, boiled, 1 each, $10^1/_2$ oz	0	6	13	60
Jerusalem, peeled, raw, 1 cup	2	0	26	114

BABY FOODS

Milk from the breast or bottle is the only food a baby needs in the first months of life. Solid foods should not be introduced too early—preferably not before 6 months—but some hungry babies will need to start solids sooner.

Solid foods

The first solid food given is often baby cereal, mixed with the baby's usual milk, or puréed fruit or vegetables. Puréed foods can be frozen in an ice cube tray, and then one or two cubes reheated thoroughly when needed. Home-cooked food should be prepared without salt and spices. Retail baby foods are usually ready-to-serve.

Fat and fiber

Babies and very small children need energy for growth and development. Fat is an important nutrient and should not be restricted at this age. Babies also need fiber but not too much because it may cause an upset stomach. However, do give fruits and vegetables to help prevent constipation.

HEALTH WARNING

Do not give babies and small children nuts, particularly peanuts. They may choke or suffer an allergic reaction.

B

FOOD	FAT g	FIBER g	CARB g	ENERGY calories
ASPARAGUS				
boiled, 6 spears	0	1	4	22
canned, 1/2 cup	1	2	3	23
AVOCADO				
raw, florida, 1 each	27	16	27	340
raw, california, 1 each	30	8	12	306
BABY FOODS (JARS)				
apple & apricots, 4 oz	0	2	15	62
apple & banana, 4 oz	0	2	14	62
apple & raspberry, 4 oz	0	2	18	66
carrot & beef, strained, 4 oz	4	2	4	64
mixed vegetables, 4 oz	0	2	8	40
pasta w/vegetable dinner, 4 oz	2	2	9	68
rice cereal w/applesauce & banana, 4 oz	0	1	19	90
pork meat-strained 2 1/2 oz	5	0	0	88
chicken meat, 2 1/2 oz	7	0	0	106
chicken & vegetable dinner, 4 oz	2	2	10	67
fruit dessert, 4 oz	0	1	18	67
BACON				
cooked, 1 oz	14	0	0	163
Canadian (see Pork)				
BAMBOO SHOOTS				
canned, drained, 1/2 cup	0.5	2	2	13
raw, 1 cup	0.5	3.5	8	41
cooked, 1/2 cup	0.5	1	2	7
BANANA				
plantain, boiled, 1/2 cup	0	2	24	89

B

BEANS

Beans contain varying amounts of protein, carbohydrate, vitamins, and minerals (see page 96). They are an excellent source of fiber, especially soluble fiber, which helps to lower blood cholesterol levels. They are also low in fat.

Cooking dried beans

Dried beans, such as red kidney beans, contain natural toxins that need to be deactivated before use. Soak dried beans for 6–8 hours or overnight; drain and in fresh water, bring to a rolling boil for 10 minutes, then reduce the heat to cook until tender.

Protein providers

Beans are an excellent source of protein, especially for vegetarians. A complete protein is made if the beans are eaten with complex carbohydrates, such as bread or rice (e.g. beans and cornbread, or chili beans and rice).

FOOD	FAT g	FIBER g	CARB g	ENERGY calories
(BANANA)				
plantain, raw, 1 each	0	2	24	90
raw, peeled, 1 each	4	0	29	110
BEANS				
adzuki, dried, boiled, 1/2 cup	0	8	28	147
beansprouts, mung, raw, 1/2 cup	0	1	3	16
blackeyed, dried, boiled, 1/2 cup	0	4	16	80
broad, boiled, 1/2 cup	0	5	17	94
green/French, cooked, 1/2 cup	0	2	4	20
green/French, raw, 1 cup	0	4	8	34
lima bean, canned, drained, 1/2 cup	0	7	20	108
navy beans, cooked, 1/2 cup	1	6	24	129
red kidney, canned, 1/2 cup	1	11	24	128
soy, dried, boiled, 1/2 cup	6	5	5	122
BEEF				
chuck roast, trimmed, 3 oz	20	0	0	282
corned, canned, 1 oz	3.5	0	0	61
dried, 1 oz	1	0	0	47
fillet steak, lean, grilled, 3 oz	7	0	0	162
flank, lean, pot-roasted, 3 oz	12	0	0	215
pastrami, 1 oz	0.5	0.5	0	27
rib, prime, roasted, 3 oz	30	0	0	348
ribeye, grilled, 3 oz	19	0	0	261
roast beef, sliced, 1 oz	1	0	0	32
rump steak, lean, grilled, 3 oz	5	0	0	143
sirloin steak, grilled, 3 oz	11	0	0	185
topside, lean, roast, 3 oz	3	0	0	132

B

BEVERAGES

Whether hot or cold, beverages help keep us hydrated. Coffee, tea, and hot chocolate are popular beverages. Cold beverages like fruit juices, fruit drinks, and carbonated soft drinks are also favorite beverages, especially among children (see page 83).

Nutritional content

Cocoa and hot chocolate contain a trace of fiber. Cocoa and tea (especially green tea) can be a good source of antioxidants and help reduce the risk of heart disease and some cancers. Though from the same plant, green tea is higher in antioxidants than black tea.

Caffeine

Caffeine acts as a stimulant and can be addictive. A small amount is a good "wake-up" because it helps us think, but too much can cause a rapid heart rate, which may be harmful. It is healthiest to limit daily intake of coffee and tea to 2–3 cups.

Low or no caffeine

Reduce your caffeine intake by switching to naturally caffeine-free herbal or fruit teas or substituting decaffeinated coffee and tea. Always check food labels for caffeine content—some is lost in the roasting process, so high-roast coffee beans are lower in caffeine than medium-roast.

Other beverages

Fruit drinks, fruit juices, and carbonated drinks may contain additives, natural and artificial. Diet or sugar-free alternatives have artificial sweeteners that reduce their caloric value.

FOOD	FAT g	FIBER g	CARB g	ENERGY calories
BEET				
boiled, peeled, 1/2 cup	0	2	8	37
pickled, slices, 1/2 cup	0	1	13	53
BEVERAGES (HOT)				
CAPPUCCINO COFFEE, 8 FL OZ				
whole milk	5	0	7	93
reduced-fat milk	2	0	7	73
fat-free milk	0	0	7	53
CHOCOLATE				
instant, low calorie, packet, dry, 1 oz	1	0	4	35
instant, regular, packet, dry, 1 oz	4	0	18	120
hot chocolate, whole milk, 6 fl oz	7	0	12	134
hot chocolate, reduced-fat milk, 6 fl oz	4	0	12	100
COFFEE, BLACK, 6 FL OZ	0	0	1	4
LATTE COFFEE, RETAIL, 8 FL OZ				
whole milk	7	0	11	140
reduced-fat milk	4	0	11	113
fat-free milk	0	0	11	80
LATTE COFFEE, ICED, RETAIL, 6 FL OZ				
whole milk	3	0	5	64
reduced-fat milk	2	0	6	52
fat-free milk	0	0	6	40
LATTE TEA, RETAIL, WHOLE MILK, 6 FL OZ	2	0	21	128
MALTED MILK, POWDER, 1 OZ	1.5	1	21	109
MOCHA COFFEE, RETAIL, LARGE, 6 FL OZ				
whole milk	8	1	16	148
reduced-fat milk	6	1	16	136

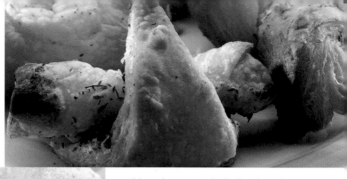

BREAD

Bread is a useful source of energy, protein, fiber, vitamins, and minerals (see page 96). Bread itself is not particularly fattening—but croissants, brioches, focaccia, and olive ciabatta may contain butter, eggs, or olive oil, creating a higher fat content.

Although you can find white bread in your local grocery store that has been fortified with calcium, iron, and B vitamins it doesn't contain the fiber.

Allergic to bread?

For allergy sufferers, there is now bread that is gluten-, wheat-, or yeast-free. These breads are made from rice, potato, beans, and gluten-free grains such as quinoa, amaranth, etc.

Whole-grain

Whole-grain breads are milled from the whole grain and are naturally higher in fiber and some minerals and vitamins than white bread. Whole-grain breads are a great way to help you reach 25–30 g of fiber each day.

FOOD	FAT	FIBRE	CARB	ENERGY
	g	g	g	calories
(BEVERAGES, HOT)				
fat-free milk	4	1	16	116
tea, black, 6 fl oz	0	0	0	0
tea, herbal, infusion, 6 fl oz	0	0	0	2
BLACKBERRIES				
raw, 1 cup	1	8	18	75
canned in heavy syrup, 1/2 cup	0	4	30	118
BLACKCURRANTS				
dried, 1/4 cup	0	2	27	102
raw, 1 cup	0	8	17	71
BLUEBERRIES				
raw, 1 cup	1	4	20	81
BOUILLON CUBES				
any, 1 cube	1	0	0.5	12
BRAN (see Cereals)				
BREAD				
bagel, plain, 1, 41/2-inch	2	3	59	303
breadsticks, 1, 7 5/8 × 5/8-inch	1	0	7	41
croissant, 1 large	14	2	31	272
raisin, cinnamon, 1 slice, 1 oz	2.5	2	14	80
focaccia, 1 oz	1.5	1	14	79
French baguette, 1 oz	1	1	14	74
hamburger bun, 1 each	2	1	22	123
muffin, English, 1 each	1	2	26	134
BREADS				
pita, white, 6 1/2-inch diameter	1	1	34	165
pita, wheat, 6 1/2-inch diameter	2	5	35	170

B

BUTTER

Butter is obtained by skimming cream from milk, then churning the cream until the fat separates from the liquid buttermilk. The result is almost pure fat, with only a small amount of water and a trace of the milk solids remaining.

Nutritional content

Butter contains more than 80% fat, most of which is saturated. It contains varying amounts of the fat-soluble vitamins A, D, and E and also beta carotene. The protein, calcium, and other minerals and vitamins from the milk are lost with the removal of the buttermilk. Salt has been traditionally added as a preservative, but low-salt and salt-free butters are available and favored by bakers.

Alternatives to butter

Margarine, processed with vegetable oils and water, has a similar fat content to butter. Hard (solid) margarine contains saturated fat but soft and polyunsaturated varieties are also available. Low-fat spreads are made using the same hydrogenation process as margarine but using much higher water content. There are also many fat-free margarines available.

Trans fat

Trans fat acts just like saturated fat in the body and can raise blood cholesterol levels. Trans-fats are created when vegetable oils are hydrogenated to make them solid. Be sure to check if a margarine contains trans-fat or has the phrase "partially hydrogenated vegetable oil."

FOOD	FAT	FIBER	CARB	ENERGY
	g	g	g	calories
(BREADS)				
rye, 1 slice, 1 oz	1	2	15	83
soda, 1 slice, 1 oz	1	1	16	82
tortilla, corn, (6-inch round) 1	1	1	12	58
tortilla, wheat flour, (6-inch round) 1	0.5	2	20	73
tortilla, white flour, (6-inch round) 1	2	1	18	104
white, 1 slice, 1 oz	1	1	1	67
whole wheat, 1 slice, 1 oz	1	2	13	69
white dinner roll, 1 oz	2	1	14	84
whole wheat roll, 1 each, 1 oz	1	2	15	75
BROCCOLI				
green, boiled, 1/2 cup	0	2	4	22
green, raw, 1 cup	0	2	4	20
BRUSSEL SPROUTS				
raw, 1 cup	0.5	4	8	38
boiled, 1/2 cup	1	2	3	27
BUCKWHEAT KERNELS				
raw, 1/2 cup	3	9	61	292
BULGAR				
(cracked wheat) cooked, 1/2 cup	0.5	4	17	76
BUTTER				
salted, 1 tsp	4	0	0	34
ghee, 1 oz	28.5	0	0	249
margarine, 1 tsp	4	0	0	34
CABBAGE				
Chinese, raw, shredded, 1 cup	0	1	2	10
green, boiled, 1/2 cup	0	2	2	13

C

CAKES

Cakes come in all shapes and sizes—some may be very high in fat and sugar while others are relatively low-fat. Enjoying a slice of cake is a treat, and a good way to help maintain a healthy weight is to choose small portion sizes.

Low-fat choices

Remember there are no "bad" foods, only bad diets. If you find it difficult to resist cakes but want to improve your diet, experiment with low-fat recipes or choose low-fat cakes when you shop. Aim for healthy ingredients, too, such as fruit or whole-grain flour. Try a low-fat date loaf, for instance. Though this may be high in sugar, it may also be high in fiber.

Nutritional content

While the majority of cakes are concentrated sources of fat and sugar, some varieties provide a good source of nutrition.

A traditional fruitcake, packed with dried fruit, contains some minerals and vitamins such as vitamins A and D.

FOOD	FAT g	FIBER g	CARB g	ENERGY calories
(CABBAGE)				
green, raw, 1/2 cup	0	2	3	2
red, boiled, 1/2 cup	0	2	2	11
red, raw, shredded, 1 cup	0	2	3	15
CAKES/PASTRIES/BUNS				
angel food, 1 slice	3	0	29	129
carrot cake, soft cheese topping, 1 piece	27	2	46	437
cheesecake, 1/6 slice	18	0	20	257
chocolate, sponge, without icing, 1 slice	4	1	36	197
chocolate, with chocolate icing, 1 slice	11	2	35	235
Danish fruit pastry, 1 each	16	0	45	335
éclair, cream-filled, 1 each, 5 × 2-inch	16	1	24	262
fruitcake, plain, 1 slice	4	2	27	139
german chocolate, 1 piece	16	2	37	300
gingerbread, 1 piece	12	1	36	263
Greek pastry (baklava), 1 piece, 2 × 2 × 2 1/2-inch	23	2	29	336
muffin, blueberry, 1 large, 3 1/4 × 2 3/4-inch	5	2	34	197
muffin, chocolate chip, 1 large	9	1	33	230
rice crispie bar, 1 oz	3	0	20	107
yellow, with vanilla frosting, 1/8 piece	9	0	38	239
CARROTS				
canned, 1/2 cup	0	1	4	18
raw baby, 2 oz	0	1	4	24
raw, 1 med.	0	2	4	22
boiled, 1/2 cup	0	2	3	19

C

CEREALS, BREAKFAST

Breakfast cereals are a good way to start the day and make a useful snack. Choose varieties that have 5 g of fiber or more and get a jumpstart on your daily fiber needs.

A balanced breakfast

All breakfast cereals contain some fiber, but whole-grain varieties have greater amounts. A bowl of whole-grain cereal with skim or reduced-fat milk, plus a piece of fruit or a glass of fruit juice, provides a well-balanced breakfast.

Added nutrition

Many cereals are fortified with vitamins such as the important B vitamins and minerals such as iron. Some cereals are also fortified with vitamin D, which can be a useful source in the winter months when its natural source (sunlight) is lacking.

Added sugar and salt

Choose cereals with little or no added sugar or salt. To sweeten your cereals, choose natural sweeteners such as fruit or yogurt.

C

FOOD	FAT	FIBER	CARB	ENERGY
	g	g	g	calories
CAULIFLOWER				
boiled, 1/2 cup	0	1	1	17
raw, 1 cup	0	2	4	34
CELERIAC				
boiled, 1/2 cup	0	1	8	32
raw, 1 cup	0	3	14	60
CELERY				
boiled, 1/2 cup	0	2	0.5	6
raw, 1 stalk	0	0.5	0.5	2
CEREALS/BARS				
blueberry, fat free, 1 bar	0	3	26	110
peanut butter & chocolate, 1 bar	5	1	22	150
strawberry, vanilla yogurt, 1 bar	4	6	53	280
CEREALS/BREAKFAST				
bran, natural wheat, 1 oz	1.5	9	7	47
bran flakes, 1 oz	5	5	19	86
bran flakes, oat, 1 oz	1	4	22	103
chocolate-flavored rice pops, 1 oz	0.5	0.5	25	105
corn flakes, 1 oz	0.5	1	24	97
fruit & fiber flakes, 1 oz	1.5	3	20	96
grapenuts, 1 oz	0	2	22	95
muesli, 1 oz	2	2.5	19	106
puffed wheat, 1 oz	0.5	2.5	20	92
puffed rice, 1 oz	0	0.5	26	105
quick-cook oatmeal dry, 1/2 cup	2	3	22	130
shredded wheat biscuits, 1 oz	1.5	7	48	229
sugar-coated puffed rice, 1 oz	0.5	1.5	23	88

C

CHEESE

Cheese is made and eaten in nearly every country in the world. Most is made from cows' milk, but goat and sheep cheeses are also widely available. There are even dairy-free cheeses available such as soy.

Nutritional content

Cheese retains most of the protein, fat, vitamin A, and calcium from the milk used to make it. Full-fat milk cheese has high-fat content and no carbohydrate. A hard cheese like Edam has a slightly lower fat content. Lower fat Cheddar-type cheeses are also made. However, salt is an important added ingredient to hard cheeses. Softer cheeses like Brie are lower in fat and soft, unripened cottage cheese can be very low-fat. Soft cheeses are also lower in salt than hard cheese. However, pregnant women and the elderly are advised to avoid all unpasteurized soft cheeses.

Alternative cheeses

Alternative cheeses made with non-animal rennet are available for vegetarians. People who are sensitive to cows' milk can enjoy cheeses made from the milk of other animals, such as goats and sheep. Dairy-free cheeses are typically made from soy beans or almonds.

FOOD	FAT	FIBER	CARB	ENERGY
	g	g	g	calories

CHARD
Swiss, cooked, 1/2 cup	0	2	3	18
raw, 1 cup	0	0.5	1	6

CHEESE
Brie, 1 1/2 oz	12	0	0	141
Camembert, 1 1/2 oz	11	0	0	131
Cheddar type, 1 1/2 oz	15	0	0	182
cottage, plain, full fat, 1/2 cup	5	0	3	108
cottage, plain, reduced fat, 1/2 cup	2	0	4	102
cottage, plain, fat-free, 1/2 cup	0	0	2	96
cream, full-fat, 1 oz	13	0	0	120
cream, low-fat, 1 oz	5	0	2	65
cream, fat-free, 1 oz	0	0	2	30
Danish blue, 1 1/2 oz	12	0	0	141
Edam, 1 1/2 oz	11	0	0	146
Edam-type, reduced fat, 1 1/2 oz	4	0	0	101
feta, 1 1/2 oz	9	0	0	108
goat, soft, 1 oz	7	0	0.5	80
Gouda, 1 1/2 oz	13	0	0	165
Gruyère, 1 1/2 oz	14	0	0	180
Jarlsberg, 1 1/2 oz	12	0	0	158
mozzarella, 1 1/2 oz	8	0	0	118
Parmesan, 1 1/2 oz	14	0	0	185
processed American, 1 oz	7.5	0	0.5	80
ricotta, 1 oz	4	0	1	58
Roquefort, 1 1/2 oz	14	0	0	165
soy, 1 1/2 oz	12	0	0	128

CHICKEN

This inexpensive meat is easily available: fresh or frozen, in portions, or whole. Choose from standard chickens to free-range and organic.

Fat

Most of the fat in chicken is contained in the skin. Once the skin is removed, the chicken flesh is very low in fat, delicate in flavor, and very versatile in terms of cooking. Light (breast) meat is lower in fat than dark (leg and thigh) meat. Some of the fat in the chicken skin is lost during cooking—pour the fat off roast chicken or grill portions on a rack so that the fat drains away.

Grilling

To grill skinless chicken, try lining the grill with non-stick aluminum foil and baste the meat with lemon juice instead of oil.

Convenience foods

Breaded and deep-fried, or spit-roasted and basted with lots of oil are sources of extra calories from fat.

HEALTH WARNING

Chicken can carry the salmonella bacteria, so the meat must be stored and cooked properly. Frozen chicken should be completely thawed before cooking and all chicken should be cooked thoroughly to an internal temperature of 165°C (330°F) before serving.

FOOD	FAT	FIBER	CARB	ENERGY
	g	g	g	calories
(CHEESE)				
spread, low-fat, with chives, 1 oz	5	0	1	54
spread, reduced-fat, plain, 1 oz	2	0	1	37
Stilton, blue, 1¹/₂ oz	16	0	0	187
CHERRIES				
canned in heavy syrup, ¹/₂ cup	0	1	38	149
raw, ¹/₂ cup	0	1.5	11	45
CHICKEN				
breast, grilled, with skin, 3 oz	5	0	0	149
breast, grilled, without skin, 3 oz	2.5	0	0	127
breast strips, stir-fried, 3 oz	4.5	0	0	138
dark meat, roasted, 3 oz	9.5	0	0	169
drumstick, with skin, (with bone) 3 oz	7	0	0	109
drumstick, meat only, 3 oz	4	0	0	80
light meat, roasted, 3 oz	3.5	0	0	132
portion, fried, dark meat, skin & bone, 3 oz	7	0	0	108
portion, fried, white meat, skin & bone, 3 oz	4	0	0	120
CHICKPEAS				
canned, ¹/₂ cup	1	5	27	143
CHICORY				
raw, 1 cup	0	2	16	66
CHILI PEPPERS				
hot green or red, raw, 1 each	0	1	4	18
jalapeno, 1 each	0	0	1	4
powder, 1 tsp	1	0	0	0
CHIVES				
fresh, 2 tbsp	0	1	2	12

C

CHOCOLATE

First consumed as a fairly bitter-tasting hot drink, chocolate has developed into confectionery, an ingredient in cakes and desserts, and an addiction for many of us!

Dark, milk, and white chocolate have varying amounts of added sugar, with white chocolate the highest. Cocoa powder has no added sugar, but some drinking chocolate powders include high sugar content. There is some iron in chocolate—it is highest in dark chocolate and cocoa and lowest in white.

HEALTH WARNING

Chocolate can trigger migraines in some sufferers. It also has mildly stimulating properties.

Nutritional content

All types of chocolate are high in fat, which is mostly saturated. Dark chocolate is the lowest in fat and has the highest amount of phytochemicals. Adding nuts to chocolate increases the fiber and the taste.

FOOD	FAT	FIBER	CARB	ENERGY
	g	g	g	calories

CHOCOLATE

coated malted milk balls, 1 oz	8	1	18	141
coated raisins, 1 oz	4	1	19	111
dark, 1 oz	9	3	17	153
expresso beans, 1 oz	7	1	16	128
milk, 1 oz	9	1	17	153
white, 1 oz	9	0	16	162

CHUTNEY, PICKLES & RELISHES

dill pickle, 1, 4-inch long	0	2	6	24
mango chutney, oily, 1 oz	3	0	14	81
sweet pickle, 1 each, 2¹/₂-inch long	0	0	5	18

COCOA

| powder, 1 tbsp | 1 | 2 | 3 | 12 |

COOKIES

animal crackers, 1	0	0	1	6
butter, 1	1	0	3	23
chocolate chip, 1 small	4	0.5	9	69
crème-filled chocolate sandwich, 1	2	0	7	47
fig bar, 1	1	1	11	56
oatmeal, 1	2	0	10	61
peanut butter, 1	4	0	9	72
shortbread, 1	4	0	10	75
sugar, 1	3	0	10	72
vanilla wafer, 1	1	0	4	28

CORN

| cob, whole, boiled, 1 ear | 1.5 | 2.5 | 12 | 66 |
| kernels, canned, ¹/₂ cup | 1 | 2 | 15 | 66 |

CREAM

Cream is made from fresh milk by skimming off the fatty layer that rises to the surface. It has high-fat content, so it should be consumed sparingly.

Fat content

The fat content of the types of cream available differs enormously:

Half & half	12% by weight as milk fat
Regular cream	19%
Whipping cream	35%
Heavy cream	40%

Lower fat choices

Sour cream and crème fraîche are made by adding a bacterial culture to cream to thicken and slightly sour it. The fat content of these options depends on the original cream used but low-fat varieties are widely available and just as delicious. Low-fat sour cream can be used as an alternative to cream in sweet and savory dishes.

Nutritional content

Cream is well known for being a high-fat, high-calorie food. The number of calories depends on the amount of fat that is present. All types of cream contain some vitamin A and D. Lower fat varieties also contain B vitamins.

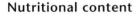

FOOD	FAT	FIBRE	CARB	ENERGY
	g	g	g	calories
(CORN)				
kernels, frozen, 1/2 cup	1	2	17	72
COUSCOUS				
cooked, 1/2 cup	0	1.5	21	101
CRACKERS				
100% stoned ground wheat, 5 pieces	3	2	14	89
cheese, 5 pieces	1	0	3	25
honey graham, 1 piece	1	0	6	30
melba toast rounds, 5 pieces	0	1	11	59
oyster, 5 each, 5 pieces	1	0	4	22
rye wafers, 1 piece	0	3	9	37
saltine, 5 pieces	2	0	11	65
thin wheat, 5 pieces	2	0	6	47
water, 5 pieces	0	1	10	44
CRANBERRY				
raw, 1 cup	0	2	1	7
juice, 3/4 cup	0	0	27	41
sauce, 1 oz	0	0	11	41
CREAM				
half & half, 2 tbsp	3	0	1	39
heavy whipping, 2 tbsp	11	0	1	103
light whipping, 2 tbsp	9	0	1	87
UHT, spray can, 2 tbsp	10	0	2	100
CROISSANT				
plain, see Breads				
chocolate-filled, 1	12	1.5	23	216

D

DESSERTS

If you enjoy eating sweet foods you may find it hard to resist the tempting array of desserts that are now available, either on the dessert cart or the supermarket shelves. Be aware that some desserts are not only high in sugar, but also in fat—pastries with cream, chocolate puddings, etc. These foods can add up calories fast so watch your portion size.

choice—try a tropical fruit salad, or baked apples stuffed with dried fruit, or pears poached in red wine.

Instead of an ice cream, have a sorbet—high in sugar but fat-free. A meringue shell (without cream) contains sugar but no fat. Accent desserts with low-fat yogurt.

Low-fat desserts

Check labels when shopping and choose low-fat desserts wherever possible. Fruit is always a good

FOOD	FAT g	FIBER g	CARB g	ENERGY calories
CUCUMBER				
raw, 1 cup	0	1	3	14
CUSTARD				
powder, with full-fat milk, 1/2 cup	5	0	23	162
powder, with reduced fat milk, 1/2 cup	4	0	24	149
ready-made, 4 oz	6	0	27	172
DATES				
dried, (with pits) 3 each	0	2	18	68
DESSERTS & PUDDINGS				
apple pie, 1/8 pie	14	2	43	296
banana split with whipped cream	65	1	124	1089
banana cream pie, 1/8 pie	20	1	47	387
bread pudding, 1/2 cup	8	1	31	219
cobbler, apple, 3 × 3-inch slice	6	2	35	199
cobbler, peach, 3 × 3-inch slice	6	2	36	203
chocolate mousse, 1/2 cup	34	0	33	447
crème caramel, 1/2 cup	4	0	25	150
frozen mousse, fat-free, 3 oz	0	1	21	72
fried fruit pie, individual, 5 × 3 3/4-inch	21	3	55	404
instant dessert, with whole milk, 1/2 cup	4	0	30	169
instant dessert, with skim milk, 1/2 cup	0	0	29	130
lemon meringue pie, 1/8 pie	14	1	41	301
rice/tapioca (whole milk) pudding, 1/2 cup	3	2	21	130
rice/tapioca (skim milk), 1/2 cup	0	0	29	140
DIPS & SPREADS				
bean, 1 oz	1	0	5	32
black bean, 1 oz	0	1	5	28

D

DRESSINGS

We think of salad as a "diet" food and most salad vegetables are very low in calories. The problem comes with the added dressing. Check the fat content on labels carefully and make low-fat dressings your first choice.

Vinaigrette salad dressing

A classical vinaigrette style salad dressing is about 3 parts oil to 1 part vinegar or lemon juice. One tablespoon of any oil (olive, corn, sunflower oil) provides 14 g fat, which is about 119 calories.

Yogurt dressing
4 tbsp low-fat yogurt
2 tbsp lemon juice
1 tbsp chopped fresh herbs
salt and pepper

Mix the yogurt, lemon juice, and herbs together in a bowl. Season to taste with salt and pepper and serve.

Spicy tomato
6 tbsp tomato juice
2 tbsp vinegar
1 tbsp grated onion
2 tsp Worcestershire sauce
salt and pepper

Mix the tomato juice and vinegar together in a bowl. Add the onion, Worcestershire sauce, and salt and pepper to taste, and mix well.

FOOD	FAT g	FIBER g	CARB g	ENERGY calories
(DIPS & SPREADS)				
guacamole (avocado), 1 oz	4	1	2	43
hummus, 1 oz	3	2	4	47
onion sour cream, 1 oz	6	0	2	63
peanut butter, 1 tbsp	8	1	3	95
salsa, 1 oz	0	0	1	5
DOUGHNUT				
jelly, 1	16	1	33	289
cake, 1	11	2	37	252
glazed, 1	13	2	28	238
DRESSINGS (see also Mayonnaise)				
blue cheese, 1 tbsp	8	0	1	77
caesar (oil/vinegar/cheese), 1 tbsp	7	0	1	69
fat free, any, 1 tbsp	0	0	1	75
Italian (oil/vinegar/lemon juice), 1 tbsp	10.5	0	0.6	89
low-fat, any, 1 tbsp	0.5	0	0	82
oil & lemon, 1 tbsp	10.5	0	1.5	89
ranch, 1 tbsp	8	0	0.5	75
thousand island, 1 tbsp	11	0	0.5	97
thousand island, reduced calorie, 1 tbsp	4.5	0	2	48
vinaigrette (balsamic or wine vinegar),1 tbsp	2.5	0	2	29
yogurt-based, 1 tbsp	5	0	1	50
DRIED FRUIT				
currants, 1/4 cup	0	2	27	102
mixed fruit, 1/4 cup	0	2	25	97
raisins, 1/4 cup	0	1	29	109

FAST FOOD

Most take-out foods—burgers and fries, pizza, fish and chips, fried chicken—are high in fat and salt. These are fine if eaten occasionally, but shouldn't be the basis of a healthy diet.

A grilled chicken sandwich or a vegetarian burger is a good low fat alternative. Baked potatoes are also low in fat but the toppings are not. Try low fat toppings like salsa instead of butter.

Being selective

Busy lifestyles can mean that fast foods are a necessity, but try to be selective and find foods that are lower in fat and contain a wide range of nutrients. A hamburger (no cheese) in a bun, with lettuce and ketchup saves many calories when eaten without fries.

FOOD	FAT	FIBER	CARB	ENERGY
	g	g	g	calories
DUCK				
roasted, meat only, 3 oz	9	0	0	163
roasted, with fat & skin, 3 oz	33	0	0	364
EGG				
egg, whole, 1 medium	5	0	0	68
fried in vegetable oil, 1 medium	11	0	0	121
large egg white only, raw	0	0	0	17
large egg yolk only, raw	5	0	0	59
omelette, plain, 5 oz	20	17	0	229
scrambled with milk & butter, 1 large	7	0	1	101
EGGPLANT				
raw, 1 cup, 82 g	2	2	5	21
cooked & drained, 1/2 cup	1	0	3	14
ENDIVE				
raw, 1 cup	0	2	2	9
FALAFEL				
deep-fried, 2 1/4-inch patty	3	1	5	57
FAST FOOD/TAKE OUT				
breaded chicken sandwich, 1	23	2	66	582
chicken breast, deep-fried, 1 piece, 3 oz	8	0	3	170
chicken nuggets, deep-fried, 3 oz	13	1	13	200
chicken strips, 1 serving	32	5	86	749
corn dog, 1	17	1	23	262
fish (e.g. cod) in batter, deep-fried, 3 oz	7	0	6	149
frankfurter in bun, plain	15	0	18	242
french fries, medium	15	0	49	350
grilled cheese sandwich	12	2	39	282

F

FISH

Fish is very nutritious and should be a regular part of family meal planning. Today there is a wide range of fish for sale, although in some parts of the world, fish is a much scarcer and more expensive commodity due to over-fishing. Fish can be roughly divided into three groups: white fish, oily or fatty fish (see page 46), and shellfish (see page 48).

White fish

White fish are saltwater fish and include cod, haddock, monkfish, sole, whiting, and many others. These fish have a very low-fat content, although the fish liver may be high in fat. If cooked without added fat, these fish are low in calories and high in protein. Cod liver oil and halibut liver oil, obtained from white fish, have very high levels of vitamin A and vitamin D.

FOOD	FAT g	FIBER g	CARB g	ENERGY calories
(FAST FOOD/TAKE OUT)				
grilled chicken sandwich, 1	13	2	31	343
hamburger, 1 large	23	0	25	400
hamburger, with cheese, 1 large	33	0	47	608
milkshake, 1 medium	10	1	60	369
onion rings, 1 medium	5	7	66	331
tater tots, 1 medium	16	3	27	259
FATS & OILS (see also Margarines)				
cocoa butter, 1 tbsp	14	0	0	120
lard, 1 tbsp	13	0	0	115
margarine, 1 tbsp	11	0	0	101
oil, any (e.g. vegetable, corn, olive), 1 tbsp	14	0	0	120
margarine, fat-free spread, 1 tbsp	0	0	0	5
FENNEL				
raw, 1 cup	0	3	6	27
FIGS				
dried, 3 figs, 56 g	0	7	37	158
raw, 1 each, 2½-inch diameter	0	2	12	47
FISH				
anchovies, 1 oz	7	0	0	83
bass, 3 oz	2	0	0	86
carp, 3 oz	4	0	0	96
clams, canned, 3 oz	0.5	0	2	66
cod fillet, baked, 3 oz	1	0	0	83
cod fillet, poached/steamed, 3 oz	1	0	0	81
cod, deep-fried in batter, 3 oz	13	0.5	10	214
cod, smoked, poached, 3 oz	1.5	0	0	87

F

FATTY OR OILY FISH

Oily fish includes herring, mackerel, eels, salmon, sardines, trout, and many others. The higher fat content in the often pink or creamy-colored flesh gives these fish a rich flavor. Their calorie content is higher than that of white fish but their flavor makes a smaller portion satisfying.

Omega 3s

Oily fish, such as mackerel, salmon, and sardines are also rich in omega-3 fatty acids. These are polyunsaturated fats and can help to protect against coronary heart disease.

Include fish high in omega 3s weekly as part of a heart-healthy diet.

FOOD	FAT	FIBER	CARB	ENERGY
	g	g	g	calories
(FISH)				
cod, smoked, raw, 3 oz	0.5	0	0	68
crabmeat, canned, 3 oz	0.5	0	0	65
crayfish, raw, meat only, 3 oz	1	0	0	58
cuttlefish, raw, 3 oz	1	0	0	61
Dover sole, raw, 3 oz	1.5	0	0	77
eel, raw, 3 oz	9.5	0	0	84
eel, smoked, 3 oz	11	0	0	144
flounder, raw, 3 oz	1.5	0	0	71
flounder, steamed, 3 oz	2	0	0	87
flying fish, raw, 3 oz	0.5	0	0	74
haddock fillet, grilled, 3 oz	1	0	0	89
haddock fillet, in crumbs, fried, 3 oz	7	0.5	9	135
haddock fillet, raw, 3 oz	0.5	0	0	70
haddock, smoked, steamed, 3 oz	1	0	0	87
halibut, grilled, 3 oz	2	0	0	104
halibut, raw, 3 oz	1.5	0	0	89
herring, dried, salted, 3 oz	6	0	0	145
herring fillet, grilled, 3 oz	10	0	0	156
herring fillet, raw, 1, 3 oz	11	0	0	161
herring, pickled, 3 oz	10	0	0	180
lemon sole, grilled, 3 oz	1.5	0	0	83
lemon sole, grilled, with bones & skin, 3 oz	1	0	0	53
lemon sole, steamed, 3 oz	1	0	0	78
lemon sole, steamed, with bones & skin, 3 oz	0.5	0	0	55
lobster, meat, boiled, 3 oz	1.5	0	0	88
mackerel, grilled, 3 oz	15	0	0	206

F

SHELLFISH AND OTHER SEAFOOD

Shellfish includes prawns, shrimps, scampi, oysters, lobsters, scallops, mussels, and many others. The total fat in shellfish is low, but all of them, particularly lobster, are high in cholesterol. Fish roe, including caviar, also has a high cholesterol content.

Cholesterol

Cholesterol is a natural constituent in the blood, and a high dietary fat intake can cause an increase in our cholesterol levels. There is some debate over the significance of cholesterol in foods, but in reality the cholesterol we take in from foods is probably much less implicated in heart disease than the type of fat we eat. It has been suggested that the cholesterol found in shellfish may not have a strong impact on blood cholesterol levels since shellfish is low in saturated fat.

Other nutrients

Shellfish contain small amounts of B vitamins and minerals, but nearly all have a fair amount of natural sodium.

FOOD	FAT	FIBER	CARB	ENERGY
	g	g	g	calories
(FISH)				
mackerel, raw, 3 oz	14	0	0	189
mackerel, smoked, 3 oz	27	0	0	304
monkfish, grilled, 3 oz	0.5	0	0	83
monkfish, raw, 3 oz	0.5	0	0	57
pompano, raw, 3 oz	2	0	0	93
striped mullet, grilled, 3 oz	4.5	0	0	129
striped mullet, raw, 3 oz	4.5	0	0	129
mullet, red, grilled, 3 oz	4	0	0	104
mullet, red, raw, 3 oz	3.5	0	0	104
mussels, boiled, without shells, 3 oz	2	0	0	89
octopus, raw, 3 oz	1	0	0	71
orange roughy, raw, 3 oz	6	0	0	108
oysters, raw, 6, 3 oz	1	0	3	56
plaice fillet, steamed, 3 oz	1.5	0	0	79
plaice fillet, grilled, 3 oz	1.5	0	0	83
plaice fillet, raw, 3 oz	1	0	0	68
pollack, Alaskan, raw, 3 oz	0.5	0	0	62
prawns, boiled, 3 oz	1	0	0	84
red snapper fillet, fried, 3 oz	2	0	0	108
red snapper, raw, 3 oz	1	0	0	77
redfish, raw, 3 oz	2.5	0	0	84
salmon, canned, meat only, 3 oz	6	0	0	132
salmon, grilled, 3 oz	11	0	0	185
salmon, raw, 3 oz	10	0	0	157
salmon, smoked, 3 oz	4	0	0	121
salmon, steamed, 3 oz	10	0	0	167

F

FISH PRODUCTS

Fish products are also nutritious and can make a valuable contribution to a good diet, as well as being an excellent way to serve fish to the family.

Fish sticks
Fish sticks are usually made from white fish, and are often very popular with children. Low-fat varieties are widely available.

Fish cakes
Fish cakes, made with white or fatty fish are another way of eating fish for those who are worried about bones or the look of fish. Fish cakes can be made easily at home, using mashed potatoes and cooked or smoked white fish, tuna, or salmon.

Canned fish
Canned fish is inexpensive and can be used for sandwiches or in homemade fish cakes. Canned tuna, salmon, sardines, and mackerel are an excellent source of vitamin D and the soft bones of salmon and sardines can be mashed into the flesh to increase the calcium content.

FOOD	FAT	FIBER	CARB	ENERGY
	g	g	g	calories

(FISH)

FOOD	FAT	FIBER	CARB	ENERGY
sardines, canned in brine, 3 oz	3	0	0	48
sardines, canned in oil, 3 oz	4	0	0	62
scallops, steamed, 3 oz	1	0	3	102
shark, raw, 3 oz	1	0	0	88
skate, fillet, grilled, 3 oz	0.5	0	0	68
skate, in batter, fried, 3 oz	8.5	0	4	143
calamari, in batter, fried, 3 oz	9	0.5	14	168
squid, raw, 3 oz	1.5	0	1	70
swordfish, grilled, 3 oz	4	0	0	120
swordfish, raw, 3 oz	3.5	0	0	94
trout, brown, raw, 3 oz	3.5	0	0	96
trout, rainbow, raw, 3 oz	4	0	0	108
tuna, canned in spring water, 3 oz	1	0	0	99
tuna, canned in oil, 3 oz	8	0	0	163
tuna, raw, 3 oz	4	0	0	117
tuna, grilled, 3 oz	6	0	0	143
turbot, grilled, 3 oz	3	0	0	105
turbot, raw, 3 oz	3	0	0	82
whiting, raw, 3 oz	0.5	0	0	70
whiting, steamed, 3 oz	1	0	0	78

F

FLOUR

Flour is made from the milling of grains, such as wheat, maize, rice, rye, and millet. In Western countries the majority of flour is produced from wheat. Flour was probably man's first convenience food and it is still valued for its versatility besides its contribution to nutrition.

and niacin, which are added back in after milling. Calcium, iron, and folic acid are also typically added.

Whole-grain flours

The composition of whole-grain flours varies. Whole-grain flour is highest in fiber and may contain more minerals and vitamins than fortified white.

Gluten sensitivity

The proteins of wheat, rye, and barley contain gluten and must be avoided by those intolerant to it. Oats contain a similar protein that does not always affect those who are sensitive to it. Nowadays, gluten-free alternatives are widely available.

White flour

White flour is an extraction from whole wheat, resulting in the loss of certain nutrients. Flour is enriched with B vitamins thiamin

FOOD	FAT	FIBER	CARB	ENERGY
	g	g	g	calories
FLOUR				
arrowroot, 1 cup	0	4	113	457
buckwheat, 1 cup	4	12	85	402
carob, 1 cup	1	41	111	225
cornmeal, 1 cup	2	10	107	505
millet, 1 cup	4	8	104	440
potato, 1 cup	1	9	95	410
rice, 1 cup	2	4	127	578
rye, whole, 1 cup	4	16	80	400
semolina, raw, 1 cup	2.5	4	98	438
soy, full-fat, 1 cup	30	13	30	559
100% wheat, 1 cup	2.5	9	86	404
wheat, white, bread making, 1 cup	2	4.5	94	426
white all-purpose, 1 cup	1	3	95	455
FRANKFURTER				
all beef cooked, 1 1/2 oz	12	0	1	134
chicken, 1 1/2 oz	8	0	3	109
tofu dog, 1 1/2 oz	3	0	28	61
turkey, 1 1/2 oz	8	0	6	96
FRUIT SALAD/COCKTAIL				
canned in juice, 1/2 cup	0	1	14	55
canned in syrup, 1/2 cup	0	1	23	91
GARLIC				
fresh, peeled, 2 cloves	0	0	1	6
powder, 1 tbsp	0	1	6	28
GELATINE				
powder, 1 oz	0	0	0	96

H

HAM

Ham is a leg of pork, which is preserved by various salting methods. Today there is a wide choice of leaner cuts of ham available from supermarkets and delicatessens. It is a good source of protein.

Salt

Because of the salting process ham has a fairly high sodium content.

Other choices

The sliced ham available is sometimes formed from lean reconstituted meat. It will have a slightly higher water content, but is still delicious. It is a good protein source, quite low in fat. It is excellent for sandwiches and salads.

Choice cut

The best and tastiest ham is carved from the bone, and is lean, pale pink and slightly dry looking. This is expensive, but perfect for salads and sandwiches. Try boiling or roasting your own ham, either boned and rolled, or on the bone for a special occasion. It is delicious hot or cold.

FOOD	FAT	FIBER	CARB	ENERGY
	g	g	g	calories
GINGER				
ground, 1 tbsp	0	1	4	19
root, raw, 1 tbsp	0	0	1	4
GOOSE				
roasted, without bones/skin, 3 oz	19	0	0	274
GRAPEFRUIT				
canned in juice, 1/2 cup	0	1	11	46
canned in syrup, 1/2 cup	0	0	14	56
juice, concentrate, unsweetened, 3/4 cup	0	0	18	76
juice, unsweetened, 3/4 cup	0	0	17	72
raw, 1 each, 4-inch diameter	0	3	21	82
GRAPES				
raw, 1 cup	0	1	16	60
GRAVY				
brown, dry, 1 tbsp	1	0	4	22
beef, canned, 1 oz	1	0	1	15
white, prepared, 1 oz	3	0	3	42
GUACAMOLE (see Dips)				
GUAVA				
raw, 1 each	1	5	11	46
HAM				
canned, 1 slice, 1 oz	4	0	0	64
dry-cured prosciutto, 1 oz	10	0	0	189
honey roast, 1 oz	4.5	0	<1	126
oak smoked, 1 oz	3	0	<1	104
Parma, 1 oz	10	0	0	187

K

KIWI FRUIT

Kiwi fruit, also known as Chinese gooseberries, grow on the deciduous vine Actinidia deliciosa *and are now widely available. Kiwi fruit are available in golden and green varieties. The fruit looks very attractive sliced in a fruit salad, but they are also delicious simply eaten peeled.*

Nutritional content

Kiwi fruit is an excellent source of vitamin C, contains some beta carotene, and is high in potassium. Most children are attracted to its vibrant color and enjoy its sweet taste.

SERVING SUGGESTION

For a low-fat dessert, make a meringue base. For a beautiful presentation, arrange sliced kiwi fruit over the top of a meringue shell and serve with low-fat vanilla yogurt.

FOOD	FAT	FIBER	CARB	ENERGY
	g	g	g	calories

HONEY

FOOD	FAT	FIBER	CARB	ENERGY
honeycomb, 1 oz	4	0	21	78
strained, jar, 1 oz	0	0	22	80

HORSERADISH

FOOD	FAT	FIBER	CARB	ENERGY
raw, 1 tsp	0	0	2	9
sauce, 1 oz	3	0	1	29

HUMMUS (see Dips)

ICE CREAM

FOOD	FAT	FIBER	CARB	ENERGY
cake cone, with 1/2 cup vanilla	16	0	46	338
chocolate covered bar, 1	23	2	36	339
dairy, vanilla, 1 bar	13	0	15	190
soft scoop, vanilla, 1/2 cup	5	0	22	140
sugar cone, with 1/2 cup vanilla	12	0	20	195
vanilla, in dish, 1/2 cup	12	0	17	178
wafflecone, with 1/2 cup vanilla	17	0	39	318

JAM

FOOD	FAT	FIBER	CARB	ENERGY
apricot, 1 tsp	0	0	13	48
blackcurrant conserve, high fruit, 1 tsp	0	0	7	29
blackcurrant, reduced sugar, 1 tsp	0	0	10	40
fruit marmalade, 1 tsp	0	0	6	21
reduced sugar, 1 tsp	0	0	3	10

JELLY (see Desserts)

KALE

FOOD	FAT	FIBER	CARB	ENERGY
curly, boiled, 1/2 cup	1	2	1	16

KIWI FRUIT

FOOD	FAT	FIBER	CARB	ENERGY
raw, with peel, 1 medium	0	3	14	56

L

LENTILS

Lentils, like beans, are a major source of protein and energy in many parts of the world. Smaller lentils, such as red, green, and brown, need no soaking and make a fast, hearty meal.

Protein

In common with other vegetable sources of protein, the protein content of lentils is improved if they are eaten with bread or rice. The amino acids of the two different proteins complement each other, so lentils eaten with bread provide a complete protein.

Nutritional content

Lentils are high in fiber and are a good source of non-heme (plant) iron in the vegetarian diet. They also contain B vitamins and zinc.

FOOD	FAT g	FIBER g	CARB g	ENERGY calories
KOHLRABI				
boiled, 1/2 cup	0	1	6	24
raw, 1 cup	0	5	8	36
KUMQUAT				
raw, 1	0	1	3	12
LAMB				
lean, roast, 3 oz	15	0	0	217
cutlets, best end, lean,				
barbecued, 3 oz	12	0	0	203
cutlets, best end, lean & fat,				
barbecued, 3 oz	23	0	0	294
leg, roast, lean, 3 oz	7	0	0	162
loin chop, grilled, lean, 3 oz	11	0	0	186
shoulder, roasted, lean, 3 oz	9	0	0	169
LARD (see Fats & Oils)				
LASAGNE (see Ready Meals)				
LEEKS				
boiled, 1/2 cup	0.5	1	1	11
raw, 1 each	0.5	3	3	22
LEMON				
curd, 1 tsp	1	0	9	42
juice, fresh, 1/2 cup	0	0	4	13
raw, 1 each, with peel	0.5	5	3	22
LENTILS				
boiled, 1/2 cup	0	8	20	115

L

LIVER

Liver is highly nutritious and makes a very tasty meal either on its own or as part of a dish. When buying, choose liver that looks bright and glossy and smells fresh. Liver is a particularly good source of iron and protein.

Nutritional content

Liver is fairly low in fat and is an excellent source of protein and iron. The vitamin A and D content is high and it is also a good source of B vitamins, particularly folate. The animal livers available are usually calf, lamb, pig, or ox. Calf or lamb's liver is the tenderest and delicately flavored, while pig and ox liver are slightly firmer and stronger tasting. Chicken livers are much smaller, but equally nutritious.

Liver pâté

Many kinds of liver are used to make this delicious pâté, though it often has a very high fat content. For people who do not enjoy eating liver in its usual form, pâté is a successful alternative. It is an excellent source of iron and other vitamins and minerals.

HEALTH WARNING

Pregnant women are advised not to eat liver, because the very high vitamin A content may be harmful to the developing baby. People who are on low-cholesterol diets should limit their intake of liver.

FOOD	FAT	FIBER	CARB	ENERGY
	g	g	g	calories
LETTUCE				
Romaine, 1 cup	0.5	1	1	9
frisee/lamb's lettuce/lollo rosso, mixed, 1 cup	0	1	2	9
iceberg, 1 cup	0	1	1	7
raddicchio, 1 cup	0	1	1	8
LIME				
juice, fresh, 1/2 cup	0	0	4	16
raw, without peel, 1 each	0	1	7	20
LIVER				
calf, fried, 3 oz	11	0	6	217
chicken, fried, 3 oz	8.5	0	2	166
MACARONI (*see* Pasta)				
MANDARIN				
(LOOSE-SKINNED) ORANGES				
mandarin segments, canned in juice, 1/2 cup	0	1	12	46
mandarin segments, canned in light syrup,				
1/2 cup	0	1	20	77
tangerine, raw, peeled, 1	0	2	11	43
MANGO				
canned in syrup, 1/2 cup	0	1	24	87
raw, 1 each	0.5	4	35	135

M

MAYONNAISE

Mayonnaise may have been named after the French general Mahon. His chef was unable to obtain butter for hollandaise sauce, so he invented this recipe that subsequently became a classic. Mayonnaise is made from egg yolks, vegetable oil, and a little vinegar. Good-quality mayonnaise is delicious but is very high in fat and calories. Best-quality mayonnaise should be gelatinous with a pale, shiny look.

Salads and sandwiches

Mayonnaise is a favorite addition to all kinds of salads. It is also commonly added to commercially prepared sandwiches since it improves texture, moisture, and flavor. If you are counting calories, check your salad or sandwich for mayonnaise—one tablespoon of mayo contains about 100 calories and 11 g of fat.

Lower fat mayo

For those looking for a lower fat alternative, "light" mayonnaise is widely available. However, despite the fact that it contains at least half the amount of fat present in the classic product, reduced-fat mayonnaise remains a fairly high-fat product.

FOOD	FAT	FIBER	CARB	ENERGY
	g	g	g	calories

MAPLE SYRUP

| 1 tbsp | 0 | 0 | 13 | 53 |

MARGARINE (*see also* Fats & Oils)

MARMALADE (*see* Jam)

MARZIPAN

| 1 tbsp | 3 | 0.5 | 14 | 81 |

MATZO

| square, 1 large | 0.5 | 0.5 | 18 | 79 |

MAYONNAISE

home-made, 1 tbsp	13	0	0	119
prepared, 1 tbsp	12	0	0	104
prepared, reduced calorie, 1 tbsp	5	0	1	50

MEAT SUBSTITUTE

| Texturized vegetable protein | | | | |
| (TVP), 1 oz | 1 | 5 | 7 | 82 |

MELON

cantaloupe-type, 1 cup	0	1.5	7	32
honeydew, 1 cup	0	1.5	11	48
watermelon, 1 cup	0	0.5	8	37

MERINGUE

| shell, plain | 0 | 0 | 8 | 30 |

M

MILK

Milk has been valued for years as an important food, especially for children. As well as being high in protein, it is also a rich source of calcium.

Nutritional content

Milk is the major source of calcium for children and adults alike, building and maintaining strong and healthy bones and teeth. Milk is fortified with vitamin A and D and contains phosphorus, riboflavin, and calcium. Milk is an important nutritional source for the elderly—the calcium it contains protects against osteoporosis.

Other types of milk

Soy or other plant milk substitutes can be used but select varieties fortified with calcium and other nutrients.

Fat content

The percent milk fat refers to the percent milk fat by weight and the calories vary. The percentage amount of fat in milk along with the fat and calories in 1 cup is approximately:

	% milk fat	fat (g)	calories
whole milk	3.25%	8	150
reduced fat	2%	5	120
non-fat	less than 1%	less than 1	85

FOOD	FAT	FIBER	CARB	ENERGY
	g	g	g	calories
MILK				
buttermilk, 8 fl oz	8	0	12	99
condensed, full-fat, sweetened, 8 fl oz	27	0	166	982
dried skim, prepared, 8 fl oz	0	0	12	82
evaporated, full-fat, 8 fl oz	54	0	26	338
goat, 8 fl oz	10	0	11	168
reduced-fat, 8 fl oz	5	0	12	122
skim, 8 fl oz	0	0	12	86
soy, plain, 8 fl oz	7	0	14	160
soy, plain, low-fat, 8 fl oz	2	0	16	100
whole, 8 fl oz	8	0	11	150
MISO				
1 tbsp	1	1	5	35
MIXED FRUIT (see Dried Fruit)				
MIXED VEGETABLES				
frozen, boiled, 1/2 cup	0	4	12	54
MOLASSES				
1 tbsp	0	0	10	40
MULBERRIES				
raw, 1 cup	0	2	11	50
MUSHROOMS				
button, cooked, 1/2 cup	0	0	2	14
button, raw, 1 cup	0	1	4	24
Chinese, enokii, raw, 1	0	0	0	2
oyster, raw, 1 large	1	4	9	55
portabella, raw, 2 1/2 oz	0	1	3	25
shitake, cooked, 2 1/2 oz	0	0	10	40

NOODLES

Noodles are available in various forms; some wheat-based noodles are similar to dried pasta, while others contain egg and are a little higher in fat. Rice noodles are slightly softer in texture and lower in protein than wheat noodles and cellophane or transparent noodles are made from ground mung beans.

Stir-fries & soups

Noodles are a good low-fat accompaniment to a stir-fry, taking only a few minutes to cook while you stir the vegetables and flavorings in the wok. They are also ideal added to a homemade vegetable or chicken broth.

FOOD	FAT	FIBER	CARB	ENERGY
	g	g	g	calories

MUSTARD

FOOD	FAT	FIBER	CARB	ENERGY
American, 1 tsp	0	0	0	3
English, powder, 1 tsp	1	0	1	14
French, 1 tsp	0	0	0	4
wholegrain, retail, 1 tsp	1.5	0	1	20

NECTARINE

FOOD	FAT	FIBER	CARB	ENERGY
raw, 1	0	3.5	14	60

NOODLES

FOOD	FAT	FIBER	CARB	ENERGY
egg, boiled, 1/2 cup	1	1.5	21	99
plain, boiled, 1/2 cup	0	1	20	99
rice, white, cooked, 1/2 cup	0	1	22	96

NUTS

FOOD	FAT	FIBER	CARB	ENERGY
almonds, shelled, 1 oz	15	4	2	166
Brazil, shelled, 1 oz	19	2	1	189
cashew nuts, roasted/salted, 1 oz	14	3	6	170
chestnuts, peeled, 1 oz	1	2	10	48
hazel, shelled, 1 oz	17	2	2	181
peanuts, dry roasted, 1 oz	13	2	3	165
peanuts, roasted/salted, 1 oz	15	2	2	169
pecans, shelled, 1 oz	21	2	2	207
pistachios, roasted/salted, 1 oz	17	3	3	168
walnuts, shelled, 6 halves, 1 oz	20	2	1	193

ORANGES

Oranges, a popular citrus fruit, originated in China, but are now cultivated all over the world. They are relatively inexpensive and are an excellent source of vitamin C.

Nutritional content

One orange provides about 14 g of carbohydrate in the form of natural sugar. Oranges also contain some fiber and they are high vitamin C content. All oranges are a good source of folate and beta carotene with particularly high levels of carotene found in red blood oranges. Useful amounts of calcium and magnesium are present in both oranges and orange juice.

Despite a low iron content, the high vitamin C level helps increase the absorption of iron from both plant and animal foods, especially eggs.

Vitamin C

The vitamin C content of fruit varies. This list shows the average vitamin C content of a range of raw fruits:

apple	1 medium	4 mg
banana	1 (6-inch)	38 mg
cantaloupe	1/2 cup	35 mg
cherries	1/2 cup	9 mg
grapefruit	1/2 of medium	40 mg
guava	1 medium	165 mg
orange	1 medium	60 mg
peach	1 medium	31 mg
papaya	1/2 medium	95 mg
strawberries	1/2 cup	45 mg

O

FOOD	FAT	FIBER	CARB	ENERGY
	g	g	g	calories

OILS (*see* Fats & Oils)

OKRA

| boiled, 1/2 cup | 0 | 2 | 6 | 26 |
| fried, 1/2 cup | 6 | 1 | 7 | 88 |

OLIVES

| in brine, pitted, 1 oz | 5 | 0 | 2 | 51 |
| in brine, with pits 1 oz | 3 | 1 | 2 | 33 |

ONION

boiled, 1/2 cup	0	2	7	29
pickled, 1/2 cup	0	1	4	17
raw, 1 medium	0	3	14	60

ORANGE

juice, fresh squeezed, 3/4 cup	0	0	19	83
juice, unsweetened, 3/4 cup	0	0	20	84
raw, 1 medium, peeled	0	3	15	62

PANCAKE/CREPE

| crepe without filling, 1 | 6 | 0 | 11 | 115 |
| pancake, plain, 6-inch diameter | 2 | 1 | 28 | 149 |

PARSNIP

| boiled, 1/2 cup | 1 | 3.5 | 10 | 52 |

PASSION FRUIT

| raw, 1 each | 0 | 2 | 4 | 17 |

P

PASTA

Pasta, such as spaghetti, penne, linguini, and fusilli is very popular as a quick and easy meal whatever the occasion. Most children like pasta and find the different shapes fun to eat.

Basic pasta

Pasta is a very useful basis for all types of dishes. It is naturally low in fat; however, some pasta dishes can be very high in fat especially if cheese or cream sauces are used.

Colored pasta

Colored pasta contains tomato purée, squid ink, or spinach to give the typical colors. These pastas may have slightly higher fiber content than white pasta.

Nutritional content

Most pasta is made from durum wheat and has a similar nutritional content regardless of shape, containing B vitamins, some fiber and iron. Whole grain pasta is higher in fiber and iron than white varieties. Fresh pasta contains more water than dried, but they are very similar nutritionally.

FOOD	FAT	FIBER	CARB	ENERGY
	g	g	g	calories

PASTA

FOOD	FAT	FIBER	CARB	ENERGY
buckwheat pasta, cooked, 1/2 cup	0.5	0	17	81
macaroni, boiled, 1/2 cup	0	1	20	99
potato gnocchi, fresh, cooked, 1/2 cup	7	1	17	134
ravioli, fresh, cheese, 1/2 cup	6	0	16	140
spaghetti, cooked, 1/2 cup	0	1	20	99

PASTA (SAUCE)

FOOD	FAT	FIBER	CARB	ENERGY
alfredo, 1/2 cup	15	1	7	200
four cheese, 1/2 cup	4	2	8	82
pesto, 1/2 cup	57	4	8	620
tomato & basil, 1/2 cup	0	1	9	43

PASTRY

FOOD	FAT	FIBER	CARB	ENERGY
filo, raw, 1 sheet (generous 1/2 oz)	0	0	12	60
puff, baked, 1 oz	11	0	13	158

PATE

FOOD	FAT	FIBER	CARB	ENERGY
liver, 1 oz	8	0	0	90
chicken with vegetables, 1 oz	1	0	0	42

PEACH

FOOD	FAT	FIBER	CARB	ENERGY
canned in juice, 1/2 cup	0	2	14	55
canned in syrup, 1/2 cup	0	1	14	71
dried halves, 3 each	0	3	24	93
raw, with skin, 1 medium	0	2.5	8	36

PEAR

FOOD	FAT	FIBER	CARB	ENERGY
canned in juice, 1/2 cup	0	2	16	63
canned in syrup, 1/2 cup	0	2	26	98
dried halves, 2 each	0	3	24	92
raw, with peel, 1	1	4	25	98

P

POTATOES

Potatoes are very familiar to us now but were not accepted as a staple food in Europe until well into the eighteenth century. Americans consume more potatoes than any other food except for milk, about 140 lb per person per year.

Potato types

The different varieties of potatoes fall into two major groups: mealy and waxy. There is little difference in nutritional content between them, but mealy potatoes are better for roasting, mashing, and frying while the waxy varieties are best for steaming, boiling, and using in salads.

Potato chips and French fries

Deep-fried potato chips are perhaps the most popular form of this tuber. The fat content of fries varies—thin French fries have a larger surface area content, so contain more fat. Thick cut fries are slightly lower in fat and oven baked contain the least.

Nutritional content

Potatoes are mostly starch but because of the comparatively large amounts eaten, they contribute more fiber, protein, iron, and vitamin C to the diet than most other vegetables. Vitamin C is stored near the skin, so potatoes are best left unpeeled or peeled very thinly.

FOOD	FAT	FIBER	CARB	ENERGY
	g	g	g	calories
PEAS				
frozen, boiled, 1/2 cup	1	6	8	55
raw, shelled, 1/2 cup	0	4	10	59
split, dried, boiled, 1/2 cup	0	8	21	116
PEPPER				
green bell pepper, cooked, 1/2 cup	0	1	5	19
green bell pepper, raw, 1	0.5	3	4	24
jalapeno, raw, 1	0.5	3	9	42
red or yellow, raw, 1	0.5	3	10	51
PINEAPPLE				
canned in juice, 1/2 cup	0	1	20	76
canned in syrup, 1/2 cup	0	1	26	99
dried, 1/4 cup	0	0	5	19
juice, 3/4 cup	0	0	26	105
raw, 1 slice, without skin, 3 × 3/4-inch	0	1	8	30
PLUMS				
canned in juice, 1/2 cup	0	1	19	73
canned in syrup, 1/2 cup	0	1	30	115
dried, 3 each	0	2	16	60
raw, with pit, 1 small	0.5	1	10	40
PORK				
skins, BBQ flavor, 1 oz	9	0	0	153
Canadian bacon, sliced, lean only, grilled, 3 oz	2	0	0	53
leg, roasted, lean only, 3 oz	6	0	0	157
loin chop, grilled, lean only, 3 oz	10	0	0	194
POTATO				
baked, flesh/skin, 1 medium	0.5	1	57	245

READY-TO-COOK FOOD & PREPARED FOODS

An essential feature of today's busy lifestyle, convenience foods have been with us for a long time—canned foods have been available since the beginning of the twentieth century, while frozen and chilled dishes are currently very popular.

Nutritional value

Most households will stock the pantry with canned goods, such as beans, pasta and sauce, tuna, fruit, and vegetables. These foods can be part of a healthy diet but remember that some nutrients are lost during the canning process.

Choices

Used sensibly, these are a great option. However, they cannot replace freshly cooked foods and it is wise to check labels carefully for nutritional value. Select low sodium varieties wherever possible.

FOOD	FAT	FIBER	CARB	ENERGY
	g	g	g	calories
(POTATO)				
boiled, 1/2 cup	0	1	16	67
chips, oven-baked, 1 oz	1.5	2	23	110
mashed, with butter & milk, 1/2 cup	4	2	18	111
new, boiled, with skin, 1/2 cup	0	1	20	80
PRUNES				
canned in syrup, 1/2 cup	0	4	33	123
dried, 3 each	0	2	16	60
stewed, 1/2 cup	0	8	35	133
juice, 3/4 cup	0	2	34	136
PUMPKIN				
boiled, 1/2 cup	0.5	0.5	2	16
QUICHE				
Lorraine, (cream, bacon, cheese), 1/8 piece	41	1	25	526
RABBIT				
roasted, 3 oz	7	0	0	168
RADISH				
red, raw, 10 radishes	0	0.5	1	6
RAISINS (see Dried Fruit)				
RASPBERRIES				
canned in syrup, 1/2 cup	0	6	28	112
frozen, raw, 1 cup	0.5	7	5	26
raw, 1 cup	0.5	8.5	6	32
READY-TO-COOK FOOD				
bean & cheese burrito, 1	9	6	66	390
beef burrito, 1	10	1	29	262
beef enchiladas w/rice & beans, frozen meal	30	8	68	634

R

READY-TO-COOK FOOD & PREPARED FOODS

We are able to buy a huge array of chilled and frozen foods and dishes. Complete meals can be bought frozen or chilled and are very convenient. However, it is worth checking whether some dishes may be more economical and as easy to make at home.

Stir-fry cooking

Stir-frying is a quick form of cooking, combining leftovers and fresh ingredients like vegetables. The standard method of stir-frying is to cook small amounts of the ingredients in a small amount of oil over high heat in a short amount of time. This brief cooking method saves time and helps retain the foods' nutrients. You can buy prepared stir-fry foods for extra convenience.

FOOD	FAT g	FIBER g	CARB g	ENERGY calories
(READY-TO-COOK FOOD)				
beef soft taco, 1	10	2	20	230
burger, vegetarian, 1³/₄ oz	2	1	2	52
cannelloni, spinach & ricotta, 15³/₄ oz	35	2	58	662
cheese enchilada w/rice & cheese,				
frozen meal	15	5	48	376
chicken burrito, 1	22	9	66	580
chicken chow mein, 12 oz	7	7	49	353
chicken kiev, 5 oz	35	1	14	427
chicken kiev, reduced fat, 5 oz	20	1	16	319
chicken pie, individual, baked, 4¹/₂ oz	23	3	32	374
chicken soft taco, 1	7	2	21	200
chili con carne, 7³/₄ oz	19	7	18	332
chow mein, 3¹/₂ oz	3	1	16	119
cod fillet, breaded, 1 fillet, 6 oz	13	3	24	304
cod fish cake, 3¹/₄ oz	8	1	15	168
corned beef hash, canned, 7 oz	18	0	12	328
egg fried rice, 3¹/₂ oz	2	1	25	149
falafel, 6 each, 3 oz	7	7	16	200
fish sticks, breaded, 3 oz	11	1	18	205
garlic bread, half baguette, 3 oz	16	2	41	342
garlic bread, half baguette, reduced-fat,				
3¹/₄ oz	8	2	41	263
gefilte fish balls, 6 pieces, 3¹/₂ oz	4	1	12	140
grape leaves, stuffed (lamb & rice), 3 rolls	13	2	7	167
hash browns, 3¹/₂ oz	7	0	24	174
lasagne, meat, 3¹/₂ oz	9	1	10	161

R

READY-TO-COOK FOOD & PREPARED FOODS

One advantage of ready meals and prepared foods is that most of them can be heated quickly in the microwave. This is a great boon for busy people, especially in a family where everybody seems to have conflicting schedules!

dishes or thawed frozen food reaches the correct temperature of 330°F/165°C, to prevent food borne illness.

For a meal in minutes that combines fresh with ready-made food, use the microwave to bake a potato to go with your shop-bought salad. Simply prick the potato with a fork and cook it on Full Power for 6 minutes, turning once. Leave the potato to stand for 10 minutes, and then it's ready to eat.

Microwave cooking

Microwaving is an excellent and safe way to cook or reheat food, but it is very important to make sure that ready-prepared chilled

R

FOOD	FAT g	FIBER g	CARB g	ENERGY calories
(READY-TO-COOK FOOD)				
lasagne, vegetable, 3¹/₂ oz	5	1	14	212
macaroni & cheese, prepared, ¹/₂ cup	7	1	15	151
macaroni cheese, canned, 7 oz	10	1	20	191
noodle, Thai-style, 3¹/₂ oz	6	1	16	142
pasta w/meatballs in tomato sauce canned,				
¹/₂ cup	5	3	14	117
pizza, deep-dish, pepperoni, 6 oz	23	3	60	485
pizza, deep-dish, sausage, 6 oz	24	0	49	471
pizza, thin & crispy, cheese, 6 oz	19	2	48	440
pizza, thin, Canadian bacon, 6 oz	21	2	35	415
pizza, vegetable, 6 oz	11	3	44	332
ramen noodles, instant beef or chicken,				
1 each	1	1	29	151
ravioli, meat, canned in tomato sauce, 8 oz	5	3	34	213
sausage biscuit, 1 each	32	1	40	485
shepherd's pie, beef, 6 oz	6	2	23	194
shrimp cocktail, 3 oz	1	2	8	81
spaghetti & meatballs, canned, 8 oz	8	2	32	236
spaghetti rings in tomato sauce, can, 8 oz	8	1	26	223
spring roll, vegetable, 1, 2¹/₄ oz	6	1	9	113
sweet & sour pork, canned, 8 oz	26	7	141	721
tortellini, fresh, meat, 3 oz	7	1	15	167
tortellini, spinach & ricotta, 3 oz	6	1	18	162
REDCURRANTS				
jelly, 1 tsp	0	0	4	17

R

RICE

Rice is a major staple for a large sector of the world's population. Brown rice is whole-grain, low in fat, and a healthier option than white rice.

Nutritional content

Rice is a source of calcium, iron, zinc, and other minerals and vitamins but in quite low levels. Much of the mineral content of rice is in the outer husk of the grain; much of this is lost in the polishing process in white rice, which removes the bran and germ where most of the fiber and nutrients are located. Although there are a number of different varieties of rice, there is very little nutritional difference between them.

Types of rice

Long-grain rice is used for most main dishes; basmati rice is particularly prized for its flavor. Short-grain round rice, used in Thailand and China, is also the rice of choice for puddings. Wild rice is actually a seed of a water grass and is higher in protein and fiber.

the pocket fat, carbohydrate & fiber counter

FOOD	FAT	FIBER	CARB	ENERGY
	g	g	g	calories

RHUBARB

FOOD	FAT	FIBER	CARB	ENERGY
frozen, cooked with sugar, 1/2 cup	0	2	37	139
raw, 1 cup	0	2	6	26

RICE

FOOD	FAT	FIBER	CARB	ENERGY
basmati, boiled, 1/2 cup	0	0	15	79
brown, boiled, 1/2 cup	0.5	1	22	102
red (wild), cooked, 1/2 cup	1	1.5	31	137
white, minute rice, boiled, 1/2 cup	0	0	17	80
white, polished, boiled, 1/2 cup	1	1	31	136

RICECAKE

FOOD	FAT	FIBER	CARB	ENERGY
plain, 1 piece	0	0	6	28

RUTABAGA

FOOD	FAT	FIBER	CARB	ENERGY
boiled, 1/2 cup	0	2	7	33
swede, raw, 1 cup	0	4	11	50

SAUCES

FOOD	FAT	FIBER	CARB	ENERGY
brown, espagnole, prepared, 1 oz	3	0	14	89
cheese, prepared, 1 oz	4	0	2	56
hollandaise, 1 oz	13	0	0	121
tomato ketchup, bottled, 1 tbsp	0	0	4	16
white, whole milk, 1 oz	2	0	1	23
Worcestershire, 1 tbsp	0	0	3	11

SAUSAGE

FOOD	FAT	FIBER	CARB	ENERGY
beef, fried or grilled, 1 oz	8	0	1	88
bratwurst, 3 oz	19	0	2	224
chorizo, 1 oz	21	0	1	258
liverwurst, 1 oz	15	0.5	5	194
mortadella, 1 oz	26	0	<1	285

S

SEEDS & NUTS

Most nuts and seeds contain protein, fat, and carbohydrate. In most seeds and nuts the fats they contains are heart healthy and an ounce a day of nuts may help lower blood cholesterol levels.

Vitamins & minerals

Seeds are high in fiber and may be a good source of minerals, B vitamins and vitamin E, relative to the quantities eaten. For example, 1 tablespoon of sesame seeds contains about 88 mg of calcium, but 1 cup of milk contains 350 mg. Milk contains 290 mg and is an easy way to meet calcium needs.

Calorie content

The nutritional value of nuts and seeds makes them a useful part of a vegetarian diet. However, they make a very high calorie snack. For example, 1 oz of peanuts contains about 14 g fat, which amounts to 165 calories.

FOOD	FAT g	FIBER g	CARB g	ENERGY calories
(SAUSAGE)				
salami, 1 slice, 1 oz	13	0	0.5	137
salami stick, 1 oz	13	0	0.5	148
vegetarian, soy protein, cooked, 1 oz	12	1	7	214
SEEDS				
poppy, 1 oz	13	3	7	151
pumpkin, 1 oz	12	1	4	148
sesame, 1 oz	14	4	7	160
sunflower, 1 oz	14	3	7	165
SNACKS				
banana chips, 1 oz	9	1.5	17	143
cheese puffs, 1 oz	10	1	15	160
corn chips (tortilla), 1 oz	8	1	17	140
pretzels, 1 oz	1	1	22	108
shoestring french fried potato chips, 1 oz	2	1	7	43
trail mix, 1 oz	8	1	13	131
SOFT DRINKS				
cola type, canned, 12 fl oz	0	0	39	152
diet (light) cola, canned, 12 fl oz	0	0	0	1
diet (light) lemonade, canned, 12 fl oz	0	0	16	65
ginger ale, canned, 12 fl oz	0	0	32	124
iced tea, sweetened, canned 12 fl oz	0	0	27	98
lemonade, canned, 12 fl oz	0	0	45	180

SOUPS

A soup can be a thin broth or a hearty meal. Homemade lentil and vegetable soup is low in fat, low in cost, and easy to make. Served with bread, it makes a good filling meal on a winter's day.

Stock

The basis for soup is often a stock, made by cooking vegetables, or meat or fish bones with seasoning and herbs, and straining off the resulting liquid. The stock gives the soup its flavor. Try to use homemade stock rather than bouillon cubes, which have little nutritional content and tend to be high in sodium.

Ready-made soups

The most nutritious soups are probably those made at home from freshly prepared produce. However, a wide variety of soups can be bought canned, dried, or fresh-chilled, which are perfect for a snack or meal. Remember to check the label for the sodium and calories one serving provides.

FOOD	FAT	FIBER	CARB	ENERGY
	g	g	g	calories

SOUPS

FOOD	FAT	FIBER	CARB	ENERGY
beef broth, ready serve, 1 cup	1	0	0	16
black bean, 1 cup	1.5	4	20	116
chicken & rice, prepared, 1 cup	2	0	7	251
chicken broth, ready serve, 1 cup	1	0	1	39
chicken noodle, prepared, 1 cup	2	0	9	75
clam chowder manhattan, as prepared, 1 cup	2	0	12	77
clam chowder new england, as prepared				
w/milk, 1 cup	7	0	17	163
cream of chicken as prepared				
w/milk, 1 cup	11	0	15	116
cream of asparagus, as prepared				
w/milk, 1 cup	8	0	16	161
cream of celery, as prepared w/milk,				
1 cup	10	0	15	165
cream of mushroom, as prepared				
w/milk, 1 cup	14	0	15	203
cream of potato, as prepared				
w/milk, 1 cup	6	0	17	148
cream of tomato as prepared				
w/milk, 1 cup	6	0	22	160
french onion, prepared,				
1 cup	2	0	8	57
gazpacho, ready serve,				
1 cup	2	0	1	57
lentil soup, as prepared,				
1 cup	2	7	22	140

S

SPINACH

Spinach is very nutritious and can be eaten as a vegetable accompaniment or added to dishes for color. Purchase spinach leaves that are dark green and vibrant.

Cooking spinach

Wash spinach thoroughly and remove any thick stalks and withered leaves. Maximize vitamins by cooking spinach in a steamer or in a microwave. Spinach can be boiled in a little water in a large saucepan and usually takes less than 5 minutes to cook. However, valuable vitamins will be lost when you throw the excess water away.

Nutritional content

Spinach is a good source of fiber and contains more protein than some vegetables. It is high in beta carotene and folate and is a source of other B vitamins. However, the iron in spinach is not well absorbed due to its oxalic acid content, which binds with the iron.

the pocket fat, carbohydrate & fiber counter

FOOD	FAT g	FIBER g	CARB g	ENERGY calories
(SOUPS)				
minestrone, as prepared,				
1 cup	2.5	1	11	82
split pea with ham, as prepared				
w/water, 1 cup	4	2	28	190
SPINACH				
fresh, boiled, 1/2 cup	1	3	1	17
frozen, boiled, 1/2 cup	0.5	1.5	0	10
raw, 1 cup	0.5	2	1	14
SPRING ONIONS				
raw, 1 cup	1	2.5	3	20
SPROUTING BEANS				
alfalfa, raw, 1/2 cup	0.5	1	0	8
mung bean, 1/2 cup	0	1	6	35
SQUASH				
acorn, baked, 1/2 cup	0	4.5	13	57
butternut, baked, 1/2 cup	0	3	11	41
spaghetti, baked, 1/2 cup	0	1	5	21
STAR FRUIT (CARAMBOLA)				
raw, 1	0.5	2	7	32
STRAWBERRIES				
raw, 1 cup	0	3	9	41
STUFFING				
herb bread, 1/2 cup	9	1	20	170
corn bread, 1/2 cup	8	1	19	160
SUGAR				
white granulated, 1 tsp	0	0	4	16

T

TOFU

Tofu is made from soy beans and is useful in the vegetarian diet as a source of protein and a basis for many dishes. Most tofu has a high calcium and magnesium content, although some varieties may have lower levels depending on the processing method. Tofu also provides some B vitamins, iron, and zinc. The fat content is fairly low in relation to the protein content.

Different varieties

Tofu can be soft and creamy or extra firm, acting like a sponge when it comes to absorbing flavors from dishes or marinades. Smoked and flavored tofu is also available.

Serving suggestion

Add tofu to vegetable soups or slice smoked tofu into a pasta sauce. It is also delicious served as a dip flavored with garlic and lemon juice.

T

FOOD	FAT g	FIBER g	CARB g	ENERGY calories
SUGAR SNAP PEAS				
boiled, 1/2 cup	0	2	7	40
frozen, boiled, 1/2 cup	0	2	8	38
raw, 1 cup	0	5	15	76
SWEETCORN (see Corn)				
SWEET POTATO				
boiled, 1 medium potato	0.5	2.5	33	96
sweet potato, raw, 1 medium	0.5	4	32	136
SWISS CHARD (see Chard)				
TAHINI				
1 tbsp	9	1	2	91
TANGERINE (see Mandarin Oranges)				
TAPIOCA				
raw, 1/2 cup	0	1	67	272
TOFU				
silken, 4 oz	3	0	3	62
extra firm, 4 oz	2	0	2	62
silken, light, 4 oz	1	0	1	42
TOMATO				
cherry, raw, 1 cup	0	0	6	23
juice, 1/2 cup	0	1	4	19
peeled, whole, canned, 1/2 cup	0	1	5	25
paste, 1 tbsp	0	1	3	13
raw, 1 medium	0	1	6	26
sun-dried, 1 oz	1	3	16	73
sun-dried in oil, 1 oz	4	2	7	60
TORTILLA (see Breads)				

T

TURKEY

Many of us think of eating turkey only at Christmas or other celebrations, but this low-fat meat is available all year round: whole, or just the breast meat. Turkey is low in fat and contains some B vitamins, iron, and zinc.

Light and dark meat

There are differences in the fat content of turkey meat. Light turkey meat (breast) without skin has a fat content of 1 g per 3-oz serving, compared to a 3-oz serving of dark meat without skin at 6 g.

SERVING SUGGESTIONS

Use cooked sliced turkey for sandwiches and salads; use turkey meat to make sweet and sour dishes or delicious low-fat casseroles with vegetables.

FOOD	FAT g	FIBER g	CARB g	ENERGY calories
TURKEY				
breast fillet, grilled, 3 oz	2	0	0	133
drumstick, roasted, with skin & bone, 3 oz	5	0	0	135
roasted, dark meat, no skin, 3 oz	3	0	0	127
roasted, light meat, no skin, 3 oz	1	0	0	114
roll, 1 slice, 1 oz	1	0	0	16
smoked, 1 oz	0.5	0	0	31
TURNIP				
boiled, 1/2 cup	0	1.5	1.5	9
turnip, raw, diced, 1 cup	0	1	8	36
VEAL				
escalope/cutlet, in breadcrumbs, fried, 3 oz	14	0	7	228
escalope, meat, no coating, fried, 3 oz	4	0	0	156
shoulder roast w/bone, lean, roasted, 3 oz	5	0	0	169
VENISON				
roasted, 3 oz	4	0	0	279
VINEGAR				
all varieties, 1 tbsp	0	0	0	4
WAFFLES				
plain, 1 each, 7-inch diameter	11	1	25	218
WATER CHESTNUTS				
canned, 1/2 cup	0	2	9	35
raw, 1 cup	0.5	2	12	57
WATERCRESS				
fresh, 1 oz	0.5	1	0	7

Y

YOGURT

Yogurt is made by fermenting warmed milk with bacteria. The nutritional content depends on the type of milk used and the fat content of the milk. All yogurts contain protein, calcium, and some B vitamins.

Live yogurt

"Live" yogurt contains active bacteria and may help to replace or maintain the natural bacterial flora of the gut. This can be valuable following a stomach upset or after use of antibiotics. Eating live yogurt may also have a beneficial effect on the immune system.

Other yogurts

Greek-style yogurt is thicker and the fat content may be higher. Yogurts are also made from sheep, goat or soy milk.

Flavored yogurts

Flavored yogurts made from cows' milk may be full-fat or non-fat with fruit, honey, or other flavorings. Sugar or a non-caloric sweetener is usually added. Be sure to check the label.

FOOD	FAT	FIBER	CARB	ENERGY
	g	g	g	calories

YAM

FOOD	FAT	FIBER	CARB	ENERGY
cooked, 1/2 cup	0	2.5	22	90
yam, raw, 1 medium	0	0.5	22	92

YEAST

FOOD	FAT	FIBER	CARB	ENERGY
bakers, compressed, 2/3 oz	0	1	3	18
dried, 1 tsp	0	1	2	12

YOGURT

FOOD	FAT	FIBER	CARB	ENERGY
fat-free, plain, 8 oz	0	0	17	127
fruit-on-bottom, all flavors, 8 oz	3	1	46	240
low-fat, fruit, 1 cup	3	0	42	225
low-fat, plain, 1 cup	4	0	16	143
non fat, fruit w/low calorie sweetener, 1 cup	0	1	18	115
very low-fat, plain, 8 oz	4	0	16	144
whole milk, plain, 1 cup	7	0	11	138

ZUCCHINI

FOOD	FAT	FIBER	CARB	ENERGY
cooked, 1/2 cup	0	1.5	4	14
raw, 1 cup	0	1.5	4	18

THE GLYCEMIC INDEX (GI)

Research into sugars and their release into the bloodstream has found that some foods behave in a surprising way when introduced into the body. It is no longer enough just to distinguish between simple sugars and more complex carbohydrates. As we are unable to predict how a food will act by its sugar and starch content alone, a table called the Glycemic Index has been drawn up to compare the release of sugar into the bloodstream that foods create against a measure of 100 for glucose. In the table, foods are categorized into high, medium, and low. High (more than 70) means that sugars are released very quickly, near to the speed of glucose itself. These foods should not be eaten on their own or they can cause a quick increase of blood sugar. They can, however, be eaten in small amounts at the same time as a food with a low score (under 55). This would equal a combined score in the medium range (55–70) and a good control of blood sugar. You should aim to include as many foods in the low range as possible for the best blood-sugar control and include those in the medium or high categories only with protein or other low-GI foods.

A low-GI diet can help to increase the body's sensitivity to insulin so that the insulin you do have works more effectively. It can also help to keep blood fats low, in conjunction with a low-saturated fat diet, and therefore reduce heart disease-related risks.

Certain foods shown in the table may surprise you in terms of release of sugars—corn flakes and parsnips, for instance, have very high scores and should be eaten with foods that bring the score down overall. Proteins and oils are not included in the Glycemic Index as they are known to be low-GI foods since they do not contain carbohydrates. Therefore, they can be eaten with the high-GI foods to slow down sugar release, for instance lean chicken with parsnips and low-GI nuts with corn flakes. You will see from the table that some "treat" foods such as ice cream and biscuits have surprisingly low GI scores, but this is often due to their high fat content and they should still be eaten sparingly.

Low-GI Foods—below 55

FRUIT AND FRUIT JUICES

Cherries	22
Grapefruit	25
Dried apricots	31
Pear	37
Apple	38
Plums	39
Apple juice	41
Peach	42
Orange	44
Grapes	46
Pineapple juice	46
Grapefruit juice	48
Orange juice	52
Kiwifruit	53
Banana	54

VEGETABLES

Broccoli	10
Cabbage	10
Lettuce	10
Mushrooms	10
Raw onion	10
Raw red bell pepper	10
Raw carrots	49
Sweet potato	54

GRAINS

Pearl barley	31
Rye	34
Brown basmati rice	52

BREADS

Mixed grain bread	48
Pumpernickel rye bread	50

PASTA

Vermicelli	35
Linguine	42
Instant noodles	47

BAKERY PRODUCTS

Sponge cake (made with egg)	46
Breakfast Cereal	
Bran cereal	42

DAIRY

Low-fat yogurt	14
Whole milk	27
Skim milk	27
Low-fat fruit yogurt	33
Custard	43

LEGUMES

Soybeans	14
Red split lentils	18
Green lentils	29
Canned chickpeas	42
Canned pinto beans	45
Green peas	48

Medium-GI Foods—55–70

FRUIT AND FRUIT JUICES

Mango	56
Golden raisins	56
Apricots	57
Raisins	64
Pineapple	66
Watermelon	72

VEGETABLES

Corn	55
New potatoes	57
Beet	64
Boiled or mashed potatoes	70

GRAINS

Brown rice	55
Buckwheat	55
White basmati rice	58

BREADS

White pita bread	58
Hamburger bun	61
Rye flour bread	64
High-fiber wheat bread	68
Whole-wheat bread	69

PASTA

Durum wheat spaghetti	55

BAKERY PRODUCTS

Pastry	59
Muffin	62
Croissant	67
Crumpet	69

BREAKFAST CEREALS

Granola	56
Porridge	61
Spun wheat cookie	69
Wheat biscuit	70

COOKIES

Oatmeal cookie	55
Tea cookie	55
Digestive cookie	59
Shortbread	64

SAVORY COOKIES

Wheat thin	67

DAIRY

Ice cream	61

LEGUMES

Fava beans	79

SUGARS

High-fruit jelly	55
Honey	58
Table sugar	64

CANDIES AND SNACKS

Popcorn	55

BEVERAGES

Orange cordial	66
Fizzy orange	68

High-GI Foods—above 70

VEGETABLES

Rutabaga	72
French fries	75
Pumpkin	75
Baked potato	85
Cooked carrots	85
Parsnip	97

GRAINS

White rice	88

BREADS

White bagel	72
White wheat bread	78
Gluten-free bread	90
French baguette	95

BAKERY PRODUCTS

Doughnut	76
Waffle	76

BREAKFAST CEREALS

Wheat bran flakes with added dried fruit	71
Puffed wheat	74
Crisped rice	82
Corn flakes	83

SAVORY COOKIES

Water biscuit	71
Rice cake	77
Puffed crispbread	81

CANDIES AND SNACKS

Corn tortilla	74
Jelly beans	80
Pretzels	81
Dates	99

BEVERAGES

High-glucose sports drinks	95

ESSENTIAL VITAMINS & MINERALS

These are the main vitamins and minerals you need. By eating a wide variety of foods, you should easily achieve your nutrient needs.

Vitamin A (Retinol)
- Helps vision in dim light and to maintain healthy skin and surface tissues. In excess it can be poisonous. Supplements should not be taken in pregnancy.
- Found in liver, fish oils, dark leafy greens, dairy, and egg yolks.

B Vitamins
- All B vitamins are essential for metabolism and enzyme systems.
- **B1** THIAMIN found in animal and vegetable foods, such as pork, eggs, vegetables, fruit, whole-grain cereals, and fortified breakfast cereals.
- **B2** RIBOFLAVIN widely distributed in foods, especially of animal origin. Milk is a particularly important source for many people.
- **B3** NIACIN is found in legumes, meat, fish, and peanut butter.

Folate (folic acid)
- Essential for cell growth, especially in pregnancy. Deficiency may lead to birth defects or a form of anemia. Found in yeast extracts, fortified cereals and grains, fruits, dark green leafy vegetables, and liver.

Vitamin C (Ascorbic acid)
- Essential for healthy connective tissue. Deficiency results in bleeding gums etc.
- Found in vegetables and fruit, especially citrus fruits, peppers, berries, and potatoes.

Vitamin D (Cholecalciferol)
- Needed for the absorption of calcium into the blood and maintenance of bones. In children deficiency of Vitamin D leads to rickets and in adults to osteomalacia.
- The main source is the action of sunlight on the skin. Natural dietary sources are all of animal origin, such as fish and animal livers and oils, fatty fish, butter, milk, and eggs. It may be added to some foods as a supplement.

Calcium
- Essential for the maintenance of bones and nerve function. Deficiency may increase the risk of osteoporosis.
- Milk, cheese, and yogurt are best sources. Calcium is also present in vegetables, fish with edible bones, and calcium-fortified soy milk. Some bread and flours are also fortified with calcium.

Iron
- Essential for the prevention of anemia.
- Present in a wide range of foods, especially animal proteins such as meat and dairy foods.

Zinc
- Helps wound healing and enzyme activity.
- Present in a wide range of foods, especially proteins—meat and dairy foods, whole-grain products, and seafood.

Healthy Recipes for You

LOSING WEIGHT SAFELY

If you're trying to lose weight, you're not alone. In 1999, statistics showed that 61% of adults in the US were classified as overweight (BMI over 25—see page 99) or obese (BMI over 30). The number of obese people in the US has doubled in the last 2 decades. Many nutritionists believe that the reason for this alarming rise is due not to our eating more, but to our doing less. Modern technology and labor-saving devices mean that we're much less active than we used to be.

Our weight is a reflection of the balance between the energy (calories) we consume and the energy we use. Our energy intake is determined by the amount and type of food we eat. Our energy expenditure is determined by a combination of our resting metabolic rate and the amount of calories we burn in day-to-day activities.

The resting metabolic rate is the amount of energy our body needs during rest or sleep. This is similar to the fuel used by a car when the engine is idling but the car is stationary.

If our energy intake equals our energy expenditure, our body weight will remain the same, but if our intake exceeds our expenditure, the excess energy is stored in the body as fat (see below).

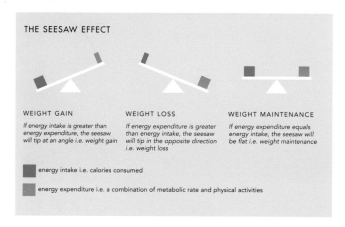

THE SEESAW EFFECT

WEIGHT GAIN

If energy intake is greater than energy expenditure, the seesaw will tip at an angle i.e. weight gain

WEIGHT LOSS

If energy expenditure is greater than energy intake, the seesaw will tip in the opposite direction i.e. weight loss

WEIGHT MAINTENANCE

If energy expenditure equals energy intake, the seesaw will be flat i.e. weight maintenance

energy intake i.e. calories consumed

energy expenditure i.e. a combination of metabolic rate and physical activities

THE IDEAL RATE OF WEIGHT LOSS

Experts agree the best and safest way to lose weight is slowly and steadily—between 1–2 lb (0.5–1 kg) a week is the ideal rate. If you lose too much weight too quickly, there is a danger of losing lean muscle tissue as well as fat. Since our basal metabolic rate (the number of calories the body needs to function) is related to the amount of lean muscle tissue we have, it's a good idea to do whatever we can to preserve it.

HOW LOW SHOULD YOU GO?

The total number of calories we need to eat each day varies, depending on a number of factors, including age, weight, sex, activity levels, body composition, and metabolic rate. As a general guide, women need around 2000 calories a day and men need 2500. To lose 1 lb (0.5 kg) a week, you need to reduce your calorie intake by 500 calories a day. Diets that restrict calories too severely (fewer than 1200 calories a day) are not recommended.

HOW YOU SHAPE UP

Although most of us can get a pretty good idea of whether we need to lose weight or not just by looking in the mirror, you can get a more accurate assessment by calculating your Body Mass Index or waist circumference (see panel below).

HOW YOU SHAPE UP

BMI (Body Mass Index) =

$$\frac{\text{weight in pounds}}{\text{(height in inches)} \times \text{(height in inches)}} \times 703$$

Below 18.5	*underweight*
18.5–24.9	*normal weight range*
25.0–29.9	*overweight*
Over 30	*obese*

For example, a person who weighs 145 pounds and is 5 feet 8 inches tall has a BMI of 22.

$$\frac{145 \text{ pounds}}{\text{(68 inches)} \times \text{(68 inches)}} \times 703 = 22$$

(Source: Centers for Disease Control and Prevention, 2003)

WAIST CIRCUMFERENCE

Men

Waist circumference over 37 in (94 cm) *indicates a slight health risk*

Waist circumference over 40 in (102 cm) *indicates a substantial health risk*

Women

Waist circumference over 31½ in (80 cm) *indicates a slight health risk*

Waist circumference over 34½ in (88 cm) *indicates a substantial health risk*

Setting unrealistic goals—if you set unrealistic goals, you're more likely to become disheartened and give up. Aim for a slow but steady weight loss of 1–2 lb (0.5–1 kg) a week. If you lose too much weight too quickly, there's a danger of losing lean muscle tissue as well as fat.

Following the wrong sort of diet—however tempting they may seem, crash diets just don't work. Although you may lose weight initially, you'll find you will end up putting on not just the weight you originally lost but more.

Not eating enough—a mistake people often make is to reduce their calorie intake too severely. Overly strict diets are difficult to stick to in the long run, they're not necessary, and they're not healthy. If you restrict your calories too severely, the chances are that you'll end up missing out on important nutrients.

UNDERSTANDING YOUR RELATIONSHIP WITH FOOD

Often we eat out of habit or to satisfy emotional needs rather than because we are hungry. We use food to celebrate, to relieve boredom, or to make us feel better when we're unhappy or lonely. Certain people, places, moods, and situations can also prompt us to eat.

Keeping a food diary will help you to identify these external cues. Buy a notebook and divide the pages into columns as shown below. Keep a record of everything you eat and drink and how you feel for 2 weeks.

FOOD DIARY					
Date and time	Where you are	What you are doing and who you're with	How you feel (e.g. tired, unhappy, bored)	What you ate	How hungry are you? On a scale of 1–5: 1=hungry 5=not hungry
Wednesday 3.30pm	*At home*	*Nothing*	*Bored*	*Package of potato chips*	*5*
Thursday 10.30am	*At work*	*Trying to meet tight deadline*	*Stressed*	*Chocolate bar*	*4*

At the end of 2 weeks, review your diary and make a list of all the triggers that prompt you to eat when you're not really hungry.

Once you have identified these trigger factors, you can start to think about solutions and ways to avoid those situations in future. Work out strategies that will help avoid or change the way you behave when faced with these triggers. If, for instance, you find you get home after work so hungry that you end up eating a family-size package of cheesy snacks while preparing the evening meal, plan ahead. Have a healthy snack such as a banana or yogurt before you leave the office so you won't feel so hungry when you get home. If your diary reveals that you use food as a way of making yourself feel better when you're unhappy or depressed, make a list of non-food related activities that will help lift your spirits when you're feeling low. Rent a video, have a manicure, or take a long leisurely bath rather than reaching for a chocolate bar.

GETTING FITTER

A combination of diet and exercise is by far the best way to lose weight. Exercise burns calories and it also helps develop muscle tissue. Muscle is metabolically more active than your body's fat stores (it uses more calories than fat). In other words, the more muscle you have, the more calories your body burns. Exercise will also help to improve your body shape and tone and help you maintain your weight loss.

If you haven't done any exercise before, take it easy when you first start. If you begin with something that is beyond your levels of fitness, you're more likely to become discouraged and give up.

Exercise doesn't necessarily mean getting hot and sweaty in the gym. Making small changes to your normal routine—such as walking instead of driving, or taking the stairs rather than the elevator—can make a big difference. Walking briskly for 20 to 30 minutes a day, 5 days a week, will burn the equivalent of 12 lb (5.4 kg) of fat in a year. Setting yourself the goal of taking 10,000 steps a day can be a good way to start.

Choose something you enjoy and that fits in with your lifestyle—you're more likely to stick with it. And try to persuade a friend or family member to exercise with you. If you make a commitment to a friend, you're less likely to back out.

The scales never lie, but they can distort the truth because muscle tissue weighs more than fat. If you're doing a lot of exercise and building muscle tissue, the scales may not move—don't be disheartened. You'll notice your body becoming more toned and shapely, your clothes will begin to fit differently as you lose inches, and—most importantly—you will be healthier.

Breakfasts

Many nutritionists consider breakfast to be the most important meal of the day, particularly for anyone watching their weight. Cutting calories by skipping breakfast is a false economy—if you miss breakfast, you're much more likely to get hungry midmorning and overeat at lunchtime. Studies show that people who eat breakfast in the morning are less likely to be overweight than those who skip it. Miss breakfast and you're also missing out on the opportunity to boost your intake of several important vitamins and minerals. People who regularly eat breakfast have been shown to have a higher intake of vitamins B_1, B_2, niacin, B_6, folic acid, B_{12}, C, and D, as well as the minerals iron and calcium, when compared with those who eat nothing. Other studies show that people who eat breakfast are less likely to suffer from colds and flu.

Dried fruit compote

prep 5 minutes + 3 hours soaking | **serves** 1

Opposite foreground: Dried fruit compote; background: Apple and blueberry granola

⅓ cup dried fruit (apricots, figs, prunes), coarsely chopped
2 cardamom pods, lightly crushed
scant ½ cup boiling water
juice 2 oranges, about ½ cup
1 tbsp fat-free plain yogurt

1. Place the fruit and crushed cardamom in a large heatproof bowl. Pour over the water and orange juice and let soak for at least 3 hours.
2. Remove the cardamom and serve with the yogurt swirled in.

COOK'S TIP
• *Any type of dried fruit combination can be used to make the compote.*

Apple and blueberry granola

prep 5 minutes + overnight soaking | **serves** 1

scant ¼ cup lowfat granola
generous ⅓ cup apple juice
1 apple, cored
½ cup blueberries or blackberries
3 tbsp lowfat plain yogurt

1. Place the granola in a bowl and pour over the apple juice, then cover and put in the refrigerator to chill overnight.
2. Coarsely grate the apple and add to the granola. Stir in the berries and lowfat yogurt and serve.

NUTRITION INFORMATION
per serving

calories	fat	sat fat
130	0.3 g	trace

NUTRITION INFORMATION
per serving

calories	fat	sat fat
252	2.6 g	0.8 g

Creamy mushrooms on toast

prep 5 minutes | **cook** 10 minutes | **serves** 1

½ tsp olive oil
1–3 scallions, trimmed and finely chopped (optional)
1 small garlic clove, peeled and finely chopped or crushed (optional)
3½ oz (100 g) whole white mushrooms (or other mushrooms, cut into fourths)
1 strip lean bacon
1 tbsp chopped fresh parsley
freshly ground black pepper, to taste
1 slice whole wheat or whole grain bread, toasted

1. Add the oil to a small, lidded, nonstick pan over low heat.
2. Add the scallion, garlic, if using, and mushrooms and stir until blended. Put a lid on the pan and continue cooking, shaking the pan to mix the ingredients. If necessary, add 1 tablespoon of water.
3. Cook the mixture for 5–10 minutes or until the mushrooms have changed color and released their juices.
4. Pan-fry the bacon quickly in a nonstick skillet and add to the mushrooms.
5. Stir in the parsley and pepper and serve on hot toast, topped with the bacon.

COOK'S TIPS

• *Add flavor by using portobello mushrooms in this recipe. Just trim off the gills before cooking to prevent discoloration.*
• *To dress this dish up for dinner, you can substitute white wine for the water added during cooking, or add a little light sour cream (1 tsp adds an extra 6–7 calories and around 0.4 g of fat to the total for the dish).*

NUTRITION INFORMATION
per serving

calories	fat	sat fat
150	6.7 g	1.6 g

Ginger fruit teabread with mashed banana

V | **prep** 10 minutes + 2 hours soaking + 2 hours cooling | **cook** 1 hour 15 minutes | **prep ahead** 24 hours | **serves** 5 (10 slices)

⅓ cup no-soak dried apricots, coarsely chopped
scant ⅓ cup no-soak jumbo golden raisins
¼ cup pitted no-soak prunes, coarsely chopped
1¼ cups strongly brewed tea without milk, left to cool
1½ cups all-purpose flour
2 tsp baking powder
1 tsp ground ginger
generous ½ cup raw brown sugar
1 medium egg, beaten

for the topping (per serving)
1 small banana, mashed

1. Preheat the oven to 350°F/180°C. Lightly grease a 2-lb (900-g) loaf pan and line the bottom with parchment paper.
2. Put the dried fruits in a large measuring cup or bowl, then pour over the tea and let stand for at least 2 hours, stirring occasionally.
3. Put the flour, baking powder, ginger, sugar, and egg into a food processor and blend for a couple of minutes, or until well mixed. Add the dried fruits and blend again until mixed.
4. Turn the mixture into the prepared pan, then level the surface and brush lightly with water. Place on the center shelf of the oven for 1¼ hours, or until cooked.
5. Let the cake cool in the pan for 10–15 minutes. Loosen the edges with a knife and then turn out onto a wire rack to cool.
6. When cool, cut off slices and serve topped with mashed banana.

COOK'S TIP
• *Any dried fruit can be used as an alternative to the apricots and golden raisins.*

NUTRITION INFORMATION

per serving

(⅕ of loaf (2 slices), topped with banana)

calories	fat	sat fat
240	1.3 g	0.3 g

Soups, salads,
and light lunches

However busy you are, it's important to make the time to sit down and enjoy a proper lunch. Tempting as it is to skip meals when you're busy, you're more likely to end up snacking on chocolate or cookies later in the afternoon if you do. Try to include at least 1 serving of vegetables and 1 serving of fruit at lunchtime. Drinking a large glass of still or sparkling water before you start eating will help fill your stomach and reduce the risk of overeating.

Carrot and cumin soup

V | **prep** 5 minutes | **cook** 30 minutes | **serves** 1 (*or 2 small appetizers*)

1 medium–large carrot, peeled and finely chopped
1 small garlic clove, peeled and chopped
1 medium–large shallot, peeled and finely chopped
1 ripe tomato, skinned (see COOK'S TIP) and chopped
½ tsp ground cumin
generous ¾ cup vegetable stock
1 bouquet garni (see COOK'S TIP)
freshly ground black pepper, to taste
2 tsp dry sherry (optional)
1 tbsp light sour cream, to serve (optional)
pinch of cumin, to garnish

1. Put all the ingredients except the sherry and sour cream in a lidded pan.
2. Bring to simmering point over high heat, then reduce the heat, put the lid on, and simmer for 30 minutes, or until the vegetables are tender. Cool slightly and remove the bouquet garni.
3. Pour the soup into an electric blender and purée until smooth.
4. Return to the pan, then add the sherry, if using, and reheat. Taste for seasoning. Serve with a swirl of sour cream, if using, and a pinch of cumin.

COOK'S TIPS
• *To skin a tomato, make a cross with a knife across the stem end and pop into boiling water for a few minutes. Drain, place the tomato in an ice bath, and then slip the skin off.*
• *To make a bouquet garni, tie a bay leaf and a few sprigs of fresh parsley and thyme in a bunch or in a piece of cheesecloth.*

PREPARE AHEAD
• *Complete to the end of step 3, then cool. Cover and refrigerate for up to 24 hours. Continue with step 4.*

NUTRITION INFORMATION
per serving
(including the sherry and sour cream)

calories	fat	sat fat
135	4.2 g	0.4 g

Spiced lentil and vegetable soup

V | **prep** 5 minutes | **cook** 50 minutes–1 hour | **serves** 1

1 tsp vegetable or olive oil
1 tsp mild curry paste
1½ cups vegetable stock
1 medium onion, peeled and chopped
scant ¼ cup dried split red lentils
1 medium carrot, peeled and chopped
1 small parsnip or potato, peeled and chopped
1 medium celery stalk, chopped
1 tsp tomato paste

1. Heat the oil in a lidded, nonstick pan, then add the curry paste and garlic and stir over low heat for 1 minute.
2. Add the stock and stir to combine, then add the rest of the ingredients and bring to a simmer over medium-high heat.
3. Reduce the heat, then put the lid on and cook for 40–50 minutes, or until the lentils are tender.
4. Remove half or all the soup from the pan (according to taste—see COOK'S TIP) and purée in an electric blender. Return the soup to the pan and reheat gently to serve.

COOK'S TIP

• By blending only half the quantity, you get a nice thick soup, which is still chunky.

NUTRITION INFORMATION

per serving

calories	fat	sat fat
280	6.8 g	0.1 g

Roast mushroom and garlic soup with whole wheat croutons

V | **prep** 2 minutes | **cook** 30–40 minutes | **serves** 1

2 large open-cap mushrooms, wiped clean
2 garlic cloves, peeled
1 slice whole wheat bread, cut into small cubes
1 tsp olive oil
¼ oz (10 g) dried porcini mushrooms
1 cup vegetable stock
1 tsp fresh thyme leaves
1 tsp vegetarian Worcestershire sauce
freshly ground black pepper, to taste
1 tsp light sour cream (optional)
few sprigs of fresh thyme, to garnish

1. Preheat the oven to 350°F/180°C.
2. Loosely wrap the open-cap mushrooms and garlic in foil and place in the oven. Bake for 10 minutes, then open the foil and bake for an additional 5 minutes.
3. To prepare the croutons, drizzle the bread cubes with the oil, then place on a baking sheet and bake for 10–15 minutes, or until golden brown.
4. Meanwhile, put the porcini mushrooms, stock, and thyme leaves in a lidded pan.
5. When the open-cap mushrooms are cooked, remove from the oven, then slice and add them to the pan with the Worcestershire sauce, roasted garlic, the mushroom juices, and pepper to taste.
6. Cover and simmer for 15 minutes over low heat.
7. Let cool slightly and purée half the soup in an electric blender for a few seconds. Return to the pan and reheat gently. Stir in the sour cream, if using, and adjust the pepper to taste.
8. Transfer to a bowl, sprinkle over the croutons and sprigs of thyme, and serve.

COOK'S TIP
• *If you can get them, try using portobello mushrooms for this recipe to maximize the flavor.*

NUTRITION INFORMATION

per serving

calories	fat	sat fat
140	5.4 g	1.2 g

Spiced chicken and apricot salad

prep 10 minutes | **cook** 10 minutes | **serves** 1

scant ¼ cup, dry weight, brown basmati rice
1 tbsp lowfat plain yogurt
2 tsp mango chutney
1 tsp mild curry paste
2¾ oz (75 g) cooked skinless chicken breast, diced
2 scallions, trimmed and shredded
½ celery stalk, finely chopped
scant ¼ cup no-soak dried apricots, coarsely chopped
1 oz (25 g) fresh baby spinach leaves

1. Rinse the rice in cold water and put in a small pan. Cover with water and bring to a boil, then reduce the heat and simmer, covered, for 10 minutes, or until just tender. Drain well, then turn the rice into a bowl.
2. Mix the yogurt, mango chutney, and curry paste together.
3. Add the chicken, scallions, celery, apricots, and yogurt mixture to the cooked rice. Stir the mixture well.
4. Serve warm on a bed of baby spinach.

COOK'S TIP
• *Brown rice adds more fiber and B vitamins, but if you prefer you can use white rice. Different types of rice will have different cooking times, so follow the directions on the package.*

NUTRITION INFORMATION

per serving

calories	fat	sat fat
290	6.4 g	1.3 g

119

Lentil and goat cheese salad

(V) | **prep** 10 minutes | **cook** 20–30 minutes | **serves** 1

scant ¼ cup dried Puy lentils
1 bay leaf
2 scallions, trimmed and finely chopped
1¾ oz (50 g) red bell pepper, diced
1 tbsp chopped fresh parsley
3½ oz (100 g) cherry tomatoes, sliced in half
1¾ oz (50 g) arugula
1¼ oz (35 g) goat cheese, sliced or crumbled

for the dressing
1 tsp olive oil
1 tsp balsamic vinegar
½ tsp runny honey
1 garlic clove, peeled and crushed or finely chopped

1. Rinse the lentils and put in a medium-size pan. Add the bay leaf and cover with plenty of cold water. Bring to a boil, then reduce the heat and simmer for 20–30 minutes, or until the lentils are tender.
2. Drain the lentils and transfer to a bowl. Add the scallions, bell pepper, parsley, and cherry tomatoes. Mix well.
3. Whisk together the oil, vinegar, honey, and garlic and stir into the lentils. Serve on a bed of arugula, with the goat cheese sprinkled over.

COOK'S TIP
• *If time is short, replace the dried lentils with 2¾ oz (75 g), drained weight, canned cooked lentils.*

NUTRITION INFORMATION
per serving

calories	fat	sat fat
220	9.3 g	3.8 g

Tunisian poached egg

(V) | **prep** 5 minutes | **cook** 20 minutes | **serves** 1

1 tsp olive oil
1 small green bell pepper, seeded and thinly sliced
1 small red or yellow bell pepper, seeded and thinly sliced
1 small onion or large shallot, peeled and thinly sliced
7 oz (200 g) canned tomatoes, chopped
1 tsp ground cumin
freshly ground black pepper, to taste
1 small egg
pinch of sweet paprika (optional)
2 mini pita breads or 1 slice whole-wheat bread, toasted

1. Heat the oil in a nonstick skillet and sauté the bell peppers and onion over medium-high heat for about 5 minutes, stirring occasionally, or until they are soft and turning golden.
2. Add the tomatoes, cumin, and pepper to taste and stir to combine, then cook for an additional 5 minutes.
3. Meanwhile, heat water in a skillet to a depth of 1¼ inches (3 cm) to simmering point, and break the egg into the pan. Keep the water barely simmering and poach the egg for 3 minutes, or until the white is cooked.
4. Serve the bell peppers in an individual gratin dish with the egg on top, sprinkle with the paprika, if using, and season to taste with pepper. Serve with warmed pita bread or toast.

COOK'S TIPS
• *Make sure the egg is very fresh, or it will not poach well.*
• *If you have time, or if you are already using the oven, you can transfer the bell peppers to an ovenproof gratin dish at the end of step 1 and break the egg into a well in the middle of them. Then cook at 375°F/190°C for 10 minutes, or until the egg is cooked but still soft.*

NUTRITION INFORMATION

per serving

calories	fat	sat fat
290	10 g	2.3 g

Thai fish cakes with sweet chili dipping sauce

prep 5 minutes + 30 minutes chilling | **cook** 6 minutes | **serves** 1 (makes 2 cakes)

for the fish cakes
3½ oz (100 g) skinless cod or haddock fillet
1 scallion, trimmed and finely chopped
¼ fresh red chili, seeded and finely chopped
¼ tsp finely chopped fresh gingerroot
1 small garlic clove, peeled and crushed or finely chopped
2 tsp lime juice
1 tbsp chopped fresh cilantro leaves
1 tsp vegetable oil

for the salad garnish
½ small carrot, peeled and finely sliced into strips
2 scallions, trimmed and finely sliced into strips
1¼ inches (3 cm) cucumber, finely sliced into strips
lime wedges, to garnish

for the chili sauce
½ tsp finely chopped fresh gingerroot
½ fresh mild red chili, seeded and finely chopped
2 tsp brown sugar
½ tsp light soy sauce
1 tbsp dry sherry

1. Put all the fish cake ingredients except the oil in a food processor and blend until smooth.
2. With wet hands, divide the mixture in half and shape into 2 fish cakes. Put on a plate, then cover and chill for at least 30 minutes.
3. Prepare the salad garnish.
4. Put all the sauce ingredients in a food processor and blend until smooth (or shake them up in a lidded jar).
5. Heat the oil in a shallow, nonstick skillet and cook the fish cakes over medium heat for about 3 minutes. Turn and cook for an additional 3 minutes, or until firm. Serve garnished with salad and lime wedges, and with the sauce on the side.

COOK'S TIP
• *Make sure the fish cake mixture is well blended to ensure the fish cakes hold their shape while cooking.*

NUTRITION INFORMATION
per serving (i.e. 2 cakes)

calories	fat	sat fat
200	4 g	0.6 g

Meat and
fish entrées

Healthy eating doesn't have to mean spending hours in the kitchen. With a little thought and forward planning, there are plenty of simple dishes that you can assemble and cook in a matter of minutes. However, if you do have the time available, preparing a meal in the evening can be a relaxing and creative end to the day. Variety may be the spice of life, but it's also the key to a healthy, well-balanced diet, so don't fall into the trap of eating the same meals week in, week out. If time is at a premium, it helps to be organized. Make sure your cupboards and freezer are well stocked and plan ahead: try to write a menu for the week at the weekend when you have a little more time. Remember, vegetables are a dieter's best friend, so supplement your entrée with plenty of vegetables or salad.

Chicken and pine nuts with saffron couscous and lemon dressing

prep 10 minutes | **cook** 10 minutes, including soaking time | **serves** 1

1–2 saffron strands
1¾ oz (50 g), dry weight, couscous
2 tsp golden raisins
½ cup boiling hot chicken or vegetable stock

for the dressing
1 tsp finely chopped fresh cilantro leaves
juice of ½ lemon
1 tsp olive oil

1 x 3½ oz (100 g) chicken breast fillet, cut into 8 strips
¼ cup corn kernels
1 tsp pine nuts
10 cherry tomatoes, cut into fourths
2 scallions, trimmed and chopped
fresh cilantro leaves, to garnish

1. Put the saffron, couscous, and golden raisins in a heatproof bowl and pour over the hot stock. Stir once and let stand for 15 minutes.
2. Meanwhile, whisk together the dressing ingredients.
3. Brown the chicken strips on all sides in a preheated nonstick skillet over high heat for about 4 minutes.
4. Reduce the heat to medium, add the corn and pine nuts and cook for an additional 2 minutes, stirring once or twice. Remove the chicken from the skillet and set aside.
5. Fluff up the couscous with a fork and add to the skillet with the tomatoes, dressing, and scallions. Heat for 1 minute, or until warmed through, stirring gently.
6. Spoon onto a plate, then top with the chicken slices and garnish with cilantro.

NUTRITION INFORMATION

per serving

calories	fat	sat fat
380	11.7 g	2.5 g

Chicken with mushroom stuffing and butternut squash

prep 30 minutes | **cook** 50 minutes | **serves** 2

for the chicken and stuffing
¼ oz (10 g) dried mushrooms
scant ½ cup boiling water
1 tsp olive oil
scant 1 cup finely chopped fresh brown-cap mushrooms
1 oz (25 g) 95% fat-free soft cheese
2 x 4½ oz (125 g) skinless chicken breasts
freshly ground black pepper, to taste
2 slices prosciutto, trimmed of any fat

for the squash
1 lb 6 oz (625 g), peeled weight, butternut squash, seeded and cut into
¾-inch (2-cm) chunks
2 tbsp chopped fresh rosemary
2 tbsp chopped fresh oregano
1 tsp olive oil

1. Preheat the oven to 350°F/180°C.
2. Wash the dried mushrooms, then pour over the boiling water and let stand for 5 minutes. Drain and finely chop.
3. Heat the oil in a nonstick pan, then add the fresh and dried mushrooms and cook over medium heat for 10 minutes, or until they are beginning to brown and any liquid has evaporated. Let cool.
4. Put the soft cheese in a bowl, then stir in the mushrooms and season to taste with pepper. Mix well.
5. Using a sharp knife, make a slit lengthwise in each chicken breast to form a pocket. Spoon in the mushroom mixture. Wrap 1 slice of ham around each breast and enclose in foil to make a package.
6. Put the chunks of squash into a roasting dish. Add the chopped herbs and pepper to taste, then drizzle with the oil. Stir to coat.
7. Place the chicken package on top of the butternut squash and bake for 30 minutes. Remove the foil and return the chicken and squash to the oven for an additional 10 minutes, or until the chicken is cooked. Serve immediately.

COOK'S TIPS

- *You can replace the butternut squash with any other type of squash or pumpkin.*
- *For a different effect, you can purée the cooked squash and serve it topped with the chicken.*

NUTRITION INFORMATION

per serving

calories	fat	sat fat
325	9.5 g	2.4 g

Spanish rice with pork and bell peppers

prep 5 minutes | **cook** 40–50 minutes | **serves** 1

½ tsp olive oil
2¾ oz (75 g) lean pork tenderloin, cut into small cubes
1 small onion, or 2 shallots, peeled and finely chopped
1 garlic clove, peeled and chopped
1 red or orange bell pepper, seeded and chopped into ½-inch (1-cm) squares
7 oz (200 g) canned tomatoes, chopped
1 tbsp chopped fresh parsley
pinch of saffron strands
scant ⅓ cup, dry weight, brown basmati rice
1 cup chicken or vegetable stock
freshly ground black pepper, to taste

1. Heat the oil in a heavy-bottom, lidded, nonstick skillet and brown the pork on all sides on high heat. Remove with a slotted spoon and keep warm.
2. Reduce the heat to medium-high, add the onion, garlic, and bell pepper, and stir-fry for a few minutes until everything is soft and turning golden.
3. Return the meat to the pan, then add the tomatoes, parsley, saffron, rice, and stock and season to taste with pepper. Stir well to combine and to break up the tomatoes a little, and bring to a simmer. Turn the heat down to low and put the lid on.
4. Simmer for 30–40 minutes, or until the rice is tender and all the stock is absorbed. (If the rice is not cooked but the dish looks dry, add a little hot water.)

COOK'S TIPS
• *A good-quality, heavy-bottom pan prevents the rice from sticking or burning as it cooks.*
• *You could use cooked ham instead of pork, but bear in mind that ham is quite salty.*
• *Brown rice adds more fiber and B vitamins, but you can use white rice or easy-cook brown rice if you prefer, following the cooking directions on the package.*

NUTRITION INFORMATION
per serving

calories	fat	sat fat
430	10.2 g	2.6 g

Beef en daube with mustard mash

prep 10 minutes | **cook** 45 minutes–1 hour | **serves** 2

2 tsp vegetable oil
8 oz (225 g) extra-lean braising steak, cut into 8 pieces
10 small shallots, peeled but left whole
1 garlic clove, peeled and crushed
1 medium tomato, chopped
scant 2 cups finely sliced mushrooms
⅔ cup red wine
scant ½ cup chicken stock
1 small bouquet garni
freshly ground black pepper, to taste
1 tsp cornstarch

for the mustard mash
2 medium mealy potatoes, peeled and sliced
¼ fl oz (25 ml) skim milk, heated
1 tsp Dijon mustard, to taste

1. Preheat the oven to 350°F/180°C.
2. Heat the oil in a heavy-bottom flameproof casserole. Add the meat and shallots and cook over high heat, stirring, for 4–5 minutes to brown the meat on all sides. Add the garlic, tomato, mushrooms, wine, and stock and tuck the bouquet garni well in.
3. Bring to a simmer on the stove, then cover and transfer to the oven to cook for 45–60 minutes, or until everything is tender.
4. About 30 minutes before the beef is ready, place the potatoes in boiling water and simmer for 20 minutes, or until just tender. Remove from heat, then drain well and put in a bowl. Add the milk and mash well. Stir in the mustard to taste and keep warm.
5. Use a slotted spoon to remove the meat and vegetables to a warmed serving dish. Cook the sauce on the stove over high heat until reduced by half. Reduce the heat, then remove the bouquet garni and check the seasoning.
6. Add the cornstarch to the sauce, mixed with a little cold water to form a paste, stirring well, and bring back to a simmer. Pour the sauce over the meat and serve with the mustard mash.

COOK'S TIP
• *You could add some ready-cooked black-eye peas, or beans, to the beef if you like. This isn't traditional, but it adds extra fiber and bulk.*

NUTRITION INFORMATION
per serving

calories	fat	sat fat
330	6.4 g	1.6 g

Chili beef with black-eye peas

prep 10 minutes | **cook** 1 hour | **serves** 1

1 tsp olive oil
1 small onion, peeled and finely chopped
1 garlic clove, peeled and crushed or finely chopped
1 small green bell pepper, chopped into ½-inch (1-cm) squares
2¾ oz (75 g) extra-lean braising steak, cut into very small pieces
1 tsp concentrated vegetable stock
2 tsp tomato paste
½ fresh green chili, to taste, seeded and finely chopped
1¾ oz (50 g) canned black-eye peas (or kidney beans), drained and rinsed
3½ oz (100 g) canned tomatoes, chopped
½ tsp chili sauce
freshly ground black pepper, to taste
¼ cup, dry weight, white rice
2 tsp chopped fresh cilantro leaves, to garnish (optional)

1. Heat the oil in a nonstick skillet and sauté the onion, garlic, and bell pepper over medium heat for 2–3 minutes, or until the onion is soft and just turning golden.
2. Add the beef and cook, stirring, until browned on all sides.
3. Add all the remaining ingredients except the rice and cilantro and season to taste with pepper. Stir well and bring to a simmer, then cover and reduce the heat.
4. Cook for 30 minutes, then check the dish for heat, seasoning, and dryness. Add extra chili sauce, very finely chopped fresh chili, or ready-chopped chilies from a jar if it is not hot enough for you, and add water if the sauce looks too dry.
5. Cook for an additional 25–30 minutes, or until the meat is completely tender. Meanwhile, cook the rice according to the directions on the package. Drain and transfer the rice to a warmed plate, then spoon over the sauce and serve garnished with the cilantro, if using.

COOK'S TIPS

• *Chilies vary a great deal in their hotness—it is always best to introduce them cautiously. You can always add more later.*
• *You can make a similar dish using cubed chicken fillet and chicken stock, but the cooking time will need to be reduced to about 30 minutes.*

NUTRITION INFORMATION

per serving

calories	fat	sat fat
445	8.5 g	2.1 g

Nasi goreng

prep 10 minutes | cook 20 minutes | serves 2

1 cup water
½ cup, dry weight, basmati rice
1 tsp vegetable or olive oil
1 small egg, beaten
1 tsp sesame oil
3½ oz (100 g) turkey fillet, cut into thin, bite-size lengths
1 medium carrot, peeled and cut into thin, bite-size lengths
4 scallions, trimmed and chopped
2 garlic cloves, peeled and crushed
1 fresh hot red chili, seeded and chopped
3½ oz (100 g) cooked, shelled shrimp
scant 1 cup bean sprouts
2 tsp soy sauce
pinch of superfine sugar
chicken stock or water, as necessary

1. Bring the water to a boil in a lidded pan and tip in the rice. Return to a boil, then lower the heat to a simmer. Cover the pan and cook until the rice is tender and all the water absorbed—about 10–15 minutes.
2. Meanwhile, heat the vegetable oil in an individual, nonstick omelet pan (or small skillet). Make the omelet by adding the beaten egg and, when almost set, fold in half, then turn out and slice thinly.
3. When the rice is nearly cooked, heat the sesame oil in a preheated wok or large nonstick skillet and stir-fry the turkey pieces for 1 minute over high heat. Add the carrot, scallions, garlic, and chili and stir-fry for an additional 2 minutes.
4. Reduce the heat, then add the cooked rice to the skillet with the shrimp, bean sprouts, soy sauce, and sugar and stir gently for 1–2 minutes. If the mixture sticks, add a little chicken stock or water.
5. Arrange the omelet slices on top and serve immediately.

NUTRITION INFORMATION

per serving

calories	fat	sat fat
385	7.3 g	1.4 g

Shrimp risotto

prep 10 minutes | cook 25 minutes | serves 2

1 tsp butter
2 shallots, peeled and finely chopped
1 celery stalk, trimmed and finely chopped
scant ½ cup, dry weight, risotto rice
freshly ground black pepper, to taste
generous ¾ cup hot vegetable or fish stock
scant ½ cup hot water
scant ½ cup white wine
5½ oz (150 g) frozen cooked, shelled shrimp, thawed
4 tsp chopped fresh parsley
1 tbsp light sour cream
dash of lemon juice
1 tsp fresh Parmesan shavings, to serve

1. Heat the butter in a medium-size nonstick skillet over medium heat. When the butter is hot, add the shallots and celery and cook, stirring continuously for 3–4 minutes, or until soft.
2. Add the rice and pepper to taste to the skillet and stir well to coat the rice. Mix the stock and water together. Add just enough of the stock and water mixture to cover the rice and continue to cook, stirring frequently, until it is almost completely absorbed. Continue adding the stock and water in this way until it is almost completely absorbed. Add the wine and continue cooking until that is absorbed.
3. Stir the shrimp and half the parsley into the risotto and heat through.
4. Add the sour cream and lemon juice, then stir and serve immediately with the cheese and the remaining parsley sprinkled over. Accompany with a large mixed side salad with an oil-free French dressing.

COOK'S TIPS

• *If using fresh uncooked shrimp, add them for the last 3 minutes of cooking.*
• *Instead of the shrimp you could use the same quantity of mixed seafood—crabmeat, mussels, squid, etc.*

NUTRITION INFORMATION

per serving

calories	fat	sat fat
340	6.4 g	1.9 g

Mediterranean swordfish sauté with tagliatelle

prep 10 minutes | **cook** 35–40 minutes | **serves** 2

1 tsp olive oil
1 red onion, peeled and finely chopped
1 red bell pepper, seeded and diced
1 garlic clove, peeled and crushed or finely chopped
large pinch of dried chili flakes
1 tsp ground coriander
1 tsp ground cumin
14 oz (400 g) canned tomatoes, chopped
1 tbsp tomato paste
scant ¼ cup red wine
freshly ground black pepper, to taste
9 oz (250 g) swordfish fillet, cubed
2 small zucchini, trimmed and thinly sliced
3½ oz (100 g) dried tagliatelle or pasta shapes, to serve

1. Heat the oil in a large, nonstick, lidded pan. Add the onion, bell pepper, garlic, chili, coriander, and cumin and cook for 5 minutes or until the onions are beginning to soften. Add the tomatoes, tomato paste, and wine and season to taste with pepper. Bring to a boil, then reduce the heat and simmer for about 20 minutes.
2. Add the swordfish and the zucchini to the rest of the ingredients and stir to combine. Bring to simmering point, then cover and cook for 10–12 minutes, or until the sauce is reduced by about half and the zucchini are tender.
3. Meanwhile, cook the tagliatelle according to the package directions, then drain. When the sauce is cooked, pour over the pasta. Serve with a green salad.

COOK'S TIPS

• Any firm white fish will do instead of swordfish—cod and angler fish are both lower in fat and calories.
• You can omit the wine if you wish and add a little fish stock or water instead (fewer calories, but the fish stock is higher in salt).
• Canned or bottled sweet bell peppers are quick and easy and give an excellent flavor, but you could use one whole yellow bell pepper instead. Seed and halve, then roast or broil it until tender before slicing.

NUTRITION INFORMATION
per serving

calories	fat	sat fat
445	8.6 g	1.6 g

Vegetarian entrées

For various reasons, more and more people are choosing not to eat meat or fish. The modern approach to vegetarian cooking and the greater variety and availability of meat-free alternatives means that many more people are choosing to eat at least a couple of meat-free meals during the week. Gone are the days when vegetarian food was considered cranky and boring. Although a vegetarian diet can be a very healthy and balanced way of eating, it often requires a little more thought and planning. The key to a healthy diet—whether you're vegetarian or not—is to eat a variety of foods. The greater the variety of foods you eat, the better chance you'll have of getting the full range of nutrients your body needs. If you cut out meat, it's important to make sure that you eat other foods that provide the vitamins and minerals you would normally get from meat. Meat is an important source of the minerals iron and zinc. If you also cut out dairy products, you'll need to ensure you get enough calcium and vitamin B_{12}.

Vegetable and potato-topped pie

V | prep 5 minutes | cook 50 minutes | serves 2

1 lb 2 oz (500 g), peeled weight, potatoes, cut into chunks
2 tbsp lowfat milk
1 tsp olive oil
1 small onion, peeled and finely chopped
scant ¼ cup dried brown lentils (see COOK'S TIPS)
1 garlic clove, peeled and chopped
1 celery stalk, trimmed and finely chopped
scant 1 cup finely chopped brown-cap mushrooms
1 medium carrot, peeled and finely chopped
scant ½ cup vegetable stock
2 tsp vegetarian Worcestershire sauce
14 oz (400 g) canned chopped tomatoes with herbs
1 tsp dried mixed herbs
freshly ground black pepper, to taste
¼ cup grated half-fat Cheddar cheese

1. Preheat the oven to 375°F/190°C.
2. Put the potatoes in a pan with water to cover and bring to a boil, then simmer for
15 minutes, or until tender. Drain and mash the potatoes with the lowfat milk. Set aside.
3. While the potatoes are cooking, heat the oil in a nonstick skillet and sauté the onion
over medium heat for a few minutes, stirring occasionally, to soften.
4. Add the lentils, garlic, and celery to the skillet and stir, then add the mushrooms, carrot,
stock, Worcestershire sauce, tomatoes, and herbs and stir everything well to combine. Bring
to a simmer, then cover and cook gently for 25 minutes, or until you have a rich sauce and
the lentils are tender. If the mixture looks too dry during cooking, add a little more stock or
water. Taste and season with pepper if necessary.
5. Spoon the lentil mixture into a two-portion baking dish and level the top. Spoon over the
mashed potato and sprinkle with the cheese.
6. Bake for 15 minutes, or until the potatoes are golden.

COOK'S TIPS

• *The lentil sauce can be also used as a topping for pasta, rice, or baked potatoes. Once made, it
can be frozen in single-portion dishes as a handy standby.*
• *If time is short, replace the dried lentils with 4¼ oz (120 g), drained weight, canned cooked
lentils and reduce the cooking time by 15 minutes.*

NUTRITION INFORMATION

per serving

calories	fat	sat fat
370	5.2 g	1.7 g

Spinach and mushroom crêpes

 **prep** 15 minutes | **cook** 25–30 minutes | **serves** 2

for the filling
2 tsp vegetable oil
12 oz (350 g) white or brown-cap mushrooms, coarsely chopped
generous ¾ cup vegetable stock
9½ oz (275 g) frozen spinach, thawed and squeezed dry
freshly ground black pepper, to taste
2 tbsp light sour cream

for the crêpes (makes 8)
1 small egg
⅔ cup all-purpose flour
1 tbsp finely chopped fresh parsley
1¼ cups skim milk
lowfat oil spray

1. First, make the filling. Heat the vegetable oil in a nonstick skillet. Add the mushrooms and cook, stirring, for about 5 minutes.
2. Add the stock, spinach, and pepper to taste. Reduce the heat slightly and cook for 10 minutes or until the liquid is thick and syrupy.
3. Meanwhile, make the crêpes. Put the egg, flour, parsley, and milk in an electric blender and blend until smooth.
4. Spray an 8-inch (20-cm) heavy-bottom, nonstick skillet with oil and heat until just smoking. Ladle a little of the batter onto the bottom of the pan and tilt until the whole of the bottom is thinly coated. Cook the crêpe for 1 minute and then flip over and cook the other side for 1 minute.
5. Put the crêpe on a plate over a pan of gently simmering water to keep warm, and continue making crêpes until all the batter is used up.
6. When the mushrooms are ready, stir in the sour cream. Spoon one-eighth of the filling into the center of each crêpe. Fold each crêpe in half and serve with steamed vegetables, such as broccoli.

COOK'S TIP
• *You can freeze any excess crêpes in single portions, then reheat them in a nonstick skillet. Just be sure to put wax paper between the crêpes prior to freezing.*

NUTRITION INFORMATION
per serving (i.e. 4 crêpes)

calories	fat	sat fat
324	10.4 g	1.6 g

Moroccan vegetable tagine

 **prep** 5 minutes | **cook** 45 minutes | **serves** 2

1 tsp olive oil
1 medium onion, peeled and chopped
1 garlic clove, peeled and chopped
½ tsp ground anise
2 green cardamom pods, "bruised" by lightly rolling with a rolling pin
½ fresh red chili, seeded and finely chopped
1¼ cups hot vegetable stock
7 oz (200 g) canned tomatoes, chopped
1¾ oz (50 g), peeled weight, turnip or parsnip, or rutabaga or pumpkin, diced
1 medium potato, peeled and diced
1 small carrot, peeled and diced
2¾ oz (75 g), drained weight, canned chickpeas, rinsed
½ cinnamon stick
1 small zucchini, trimmed and diced
scant ¼ cup dried dates, chopped
generous ⅓ cup no-soak dried apricots, chopped

for the couscous
1¾ oz (50 g), dry weight, couscous
scant ½ cup hot vegetable stock

1. Heat the oil in a large, lidded, nonstick pan over medium heat. Add the onion and garlic and sauté for about 5 minutes, or until soft. Reduce the heat, then add the spices and cook for 1 minute, stirring.
2. Add the hot stock, tomatoes, turnip, potato, carrot, chickpeas, and cinnamon and bring to a boil. Reduce the heat, then cover and simmer for 30 minutes, stirring occasionally.
3. Add the zucchini, dates, and apricots to the pan, plus a little water if needed. Replace the lid and cook for an additional 15 minutes, or until the fruit has absorbed the liquid.
4. Meanwhile, prepare the couscous according to the directions on the package using the hot stock. Fork through to separate the grains, then transfer to a warmed dish and serve with the sauce.

COOK'S TIP
• *This sauce becomes even tastier if stored refrigerated for 1–2 days before eating.*

NUTRITION INFORMATION
per serving

calories	fat	sat fat
340	4.2 g	0.5 g

Fall vegetable gratin

V | prep 10 minutes | cook 30–35 minutes | serves 1

7 oz (200 g) canned chopped tomatoes
scant 1 cup sliced closed-cap mushrooms
scant ½ cup, shelled weight, fava beans, fresh or frozen
3½ oz (100 g), peeled weight, butternut squash, cut into ½-inch (1-cm) slices,
   then cut into fourths
1 medium zucchini, trimmed and cut into ¼-inch (½-cm) slices
2 scallions, trimmed and finely chopped
freshly ground black pepper, to taste
few fresh basil leaves (optional)
½ oz (15 g) reduced-fat hard cheese, such as sharp Cheddar, or a vegetarian
   Parmesan or romano
1 tbsp fresh bread crumbs

1. Put the tomatoes, mushrooms, beans, and squash into a pan and bring to a simmer, then cover and simmer over low heat for 15 minutes. Add the zucchini and scallions and cook for an additional 5–10 minutes, or until tender, adding a very little water if the chopped tomatoes don't cover all the vegetables.
2. Season to taste with pepper and stir in the basil, if using, then tip the mixture into an individual gratin dish and smooth out.
3. Preheat the broiler to medium-high. Mix together the cheese and bread crumbs and sprinkle over the top. Brown under the broiler for 1–2 minutes, or until golden. Serve immediately.

COOK'S TIP
• *Fresh or frozen corn can be used instead of fava beans.*

NUTRITION INFORMATION
per serving

calories	fat	sat fat
180	3.9 g	1.6 g

Mediterranean vegetables
with goat cheese and penne

(V) | **prep** 5 minutes | **cook** 15–20 minutes | **serves** 1

scant ½ cup dried penne pasta
1 small red bell pepper, seeded and cut into bite-size chunks
1 small zucchini, trimmed and cut into bite-size slices
1 small red onion, peeled and cut into wedges
1 tsp olive oil
freshly ground black pepper, to taste
12 cherry tomatoes, halved
3 pitted black olives, halved
1¼ oz (35 g) goat cheese, crumbled
few fresh basil leaves, to garnish

for the dressing
2 tsp balsamic vinegar
1 tsp lemon juice
1 tsp torn fresh basil leaves

1. Put a pan of water on to boil and preheat the broiler to medium-high. Cook the pasta according to the package directions.
2. Arrange the bell pepper, zucchini, and onion on a nonstick baking sheet, then brush with the oil and season to taste with pepper. Broil for about 5 minutes. Turn the pieces and continue broiling for an additional 5 minutes, or until tender.
3. When the pasta is cooked, drain well and transfer to a serving bowl. Stir in the cherry tomatoes, olives, and the charbroiled vegetables with their oil and juices.
4. Beat together the dressing ingredients and stir into the pasta. Crumble over the goat cheese, then garnish with basil and serve.

COOK'S TIPS
• *For a change, try adding a couple of drained canned artichoke hearts or cooked fresh asparagus to the vegetables.*
• *Ideal served with a mixed green salad.*

NUTRITION INFORMATION

per serving

calories	fat	sat fat
370	11.6 g	4.3 g

Quick mushroom risotto

(V) | **prep** 5 minutes + 30 minutes soaking | **cook** 30 minutes | **serves** 1

1 tbsp dried porcini mushrooms
1 tsp olive oil
1 tsp butter
½ medium onion, peeled and finely chopped
1 small garlic clove, peeled and finely chopped
5½ oz (150 g) mixed fresh mushrooms (e.g. cremini, shiitake, white)
freshly ground black pepper, to taste
generous ¼ cup, dry weight, risotto rice
generous ¾ cup vegetable stock
scant ¼ cup dry white wine (or extra stock)
1 small zucchini, trimmed and chopped
1 tsp chopped fresh parsley
1 tsp freshly grated vegetarian Parmesan or romano cheese

1. Put the dried mushrooms in a bowl, then cover with water and let soak for 30 minutes (see COOK'S TIPS).
2. About 5 minutes before the soaking time is up, heat the oil and butter in a large, lidded, nonstick skillet and sauté the onion and garlic over medium heat for 5 minutes, or until soft. Add the fresh mushrooms and pepper to taste, then stir well and cook for 1–2 minutes.
3. Add the rice and soaked mushrooms with their soaking water, stock, and wine, if using, and stir. Cover and simmer for 20 minutes, adding a little extra stock or water if it looks dry. Add the zucchini and continue to simmer for an additional 10 minutes.
4. When the rice is tender and creamy, stir in the parsley and Parmesan cheese. Serve the risotto with a mixed salad.

COOK'S TIPS
• *Don't use flat portobello mushrooms as their juices will make the dish go black.*
• *This is an alternative and quick method to cook risotto.*

NUTRITION INFORMATION

per serving

calories	fat	sat fat
435	11.4 g	4.5 g

Vegetable korma with cardamom-scented rice

(V) | **prep** 10 minutes | **cook** 35–40 minutes | **serves** 1

for the vegetable korma
1 tsp vegetable oil
1 small onion, peeled and thinly sliced
1 small garlic clove, peeled and crushed
¼ tsp ground cumin
¼ tsp ground coriander
¼ tsp turmeric
¼ tsp garam masala
generous pinch of ground ginger
1 small potato, peeled and cut into bite-size pieces, then parboiled
    for 5 minutes
½ small eggplant, cut into ½-inch (1-cm) slices and then into fourths
1 oz (25 g) green beans, trimmed and halved
¾ cup vegetable stock
1 tsp ground almonds
scant ½ cup strained plain yogurt

for the cardamom-scented rice
¼ cup basmati rice
2 green cardamom pods, lightly crushed
⅔ cup water

1. First, prepare the korma. Heat the oil in a nonstick skillet and stir-fry the onion on medium-high until soft (about 3–4 minutes). Add the garlic and spices and stir for 1 minute.
2. Add the potato, eggplant, beans, and half the stock, then stir well and bring to a simmer. Reduce the heat and simmer gently for 20 minutes, adding more stock if the mixture looks too dry.
3. Meanwhile, rinse the rice in cold water and put in a small, lidded pan, along with the cardamom pods. Cover with the water and bring to a boil, then reduce the heat and cook, covered, for 15 minutes, or until tender.
4. Add the ground almonds for the last 2 minutes of cooking the korma.
5. When the vegetables are cooked, add the yogurt and stir well. Heat for 1–2 minutes (but don't boil). Remove the cardamom pods from the rice and serve the korma on a bed of the cooked rice.

NUTRITION INFORMATION

per serving

calories	fat	sat fat
430	9 g	1.6 g

Sweet potato curry with lentils

(V) | prep 5–7 minutes | cook 40 minutes | serves 1

1 tsp vegetable oil
3½ oz (100 g), peeled weight, sweet potato, cut into bite-size cubes
2¾ oz (75 g), peeled weight, potato, cut into bite-size cubes
1 small onion, peeled and finely chopped
1 small garlic clove, peeled and finely chopped
1 small fresh green chili, seeded and chopped
½ tsp ground ginger
¼ cup dried green lentils
generous ¼ cup–scant ½ cup hot vegetable stock
freshly ground black pepper, to taste
½ tsp garam masala
generous ¼ cup–scant ½ cup hot water
1 tbsp lowfat plain yogurt

1. Heat the oil in a nonstick, lidded pan and sauté the sweet potato over medium heat, turning occasionally, for 5 minutes.
2. Meanwhile, bring the potato to a boil in a pan of water, then simmer until almost cooked (about 6 minutes). Drain and set aside.
3. When the sweet potato cubes are sautéed, remove them with a slotted spoon and add in the onion. Cook, stirring occasionally, for 5 minutes, or until transparent. Add the garlic, chili, and ginger and stir for 1 minute.
4. Return the sweet potato to the pan with the boiled potato and the lentils, half the stock, pepper to taste, and garam masala. Stir to combine, bring to a simmer, and cover. Reduce the heat and simmer gently for 20 minutes, adding a little more stock if the the curry looks too dry.
5. Stir in the yogurt and serve with boiled basmati rice.

COOK'S TIPS

• Scratch the skin of the sweet potato to make sure it is orange-fleshed—the white-fleshed variety is not so good in this recipe.
• You could replace sweet potato with pumpkin or butternut squash.

NUTRITION INFORMATION

per serving

calories	fat	sat fat
315	4.9 g	0.9 g

Tofu and vegetable stir-fry with rice noodles

V | **prep** 15 minutes + 2 hours marinating | **cook** 10 minutes | **serves** 1

100 g (3½ oz) firm tofu, sliced into strips (see COOK'S TIP)

for the marinade
1 tsp soy sauce
1 tbsp lime juice
1 tsp chopped garlic
1 tsp chopped lemongrass
1 tsp chopped fresh gingerroot
1 tsp chopped fresh red chili

1¾ oz (50 g) dried rice noodles
1 tsp vegetable oil
1¾ oz (50 g) bok choy, coarsely chopped
1¾ oz (50 g) broccoli florets, coarsely chopped
1 small carrot, peeled and cut into thin strips
⅓ cup bean sprouts
1 tsp vegetarian Thai green curry paste
2 tbsp vegetable stock
2 scallions, trimmed and halved lengthwise

1. Put the tofu in a shallow dish. Whisk together the soy sauce and lime juice and pour over the tofu with the other marinade ingredients. If possible, let marinate for at least 2 hours (see COOK'S TIP).
2. Cook the noodles according to the package directions. Drain and keep warm.
3. Heat the oil in a nonstick wok or large skillet. Remove the tofu from the marinade, reserving the marinade, and stir-fry the tofu for 1 minute. Add the bok choy, broccoli, carrots, and bean sprouts and cook, stirring, for an additional 1 minute.
4. In a small bowl or cup, mix the curry paste, stock, and reserved marinade together. Add half to the stir-fry mixture and cook for an additional 2 minutes.
5. Add the remaining paste and marinade mix and the scallions to the stir-fry and cook for 1 minute, or until the vegetables are just tender. Serve on a bed of warm noodles.

COOK'S TIPS
• Drain the tofu and wash under a running faucet, then remove excess water with paper towels.
• Make time to marinate the tofu, as it is quite bland but takes up other flavors well.

NUTRITION INFORMATION
per serving
(not including the vegetarian Thai green curry paste)

calories	fat	sat fat
360	9.4 g	1.3 g

Vegetables
and side dishes

Vegetable accompaniments and side dishes provide the perfect opportunity to boost both the amount and variety of vegetables in your diet. Although many people automatically assume that fresh is best, frozen and canned vegetables also have much to offer. Frozen vegetables are processed within hours of being harvested, so their vitamin content is preserved. Studies show that in some cases frozen vegetables actually contain more vitamins than "fresh" vegetables, which may well be a few days old by the time we use them. The vitamins in vegetables are easily lost during storage, preparation, and cooking—to maximize your vitamin content, the golden rule is to buy the freshest produce available, then store in the refrigerator and eat as soon as possible after purchase. Once cut, the vitamin C will react with the oxygen in the air and be lost, so it's important not to prepare vegetables too far in advance of cooking and eating.

Potatoes à la boulangère

(V) | **prep** 15 minutes | **cook** 1 hour | **serves** 2

14 oz (400 g), peeled weight, potatoes, very thinly sliced
1 small onion, peeled and thinly sliced
freshly ground black pepper, to taste
generous ¼ cup vegetable stock (see COOK'S TIP)
generous ¼ cup skim milk
1 tsp butter

1. Preheat the oven to 350°F/180°C.
2. Layer the potato and onion slices in a shallow, ovenproof dish, seasoning each layer well with pepper.
3. Mix the stock and milk together and pour over the potatoes. Dot the top layer with the butter, then cover with foil and bake in the oven for 30 minutes.
4. Remove the foil and continue to cook for an additional 30 minutes, or until the potatoes are cooked.

COOK'S TIPS
• *You can use an alternative to the onion such as leeks or mixed bell peppers.*
• *You could use chicken stock instead of vegetable stock if catering for non-vegetarians.*

NUTRITION INFORMATION

per serving

calories	fat	sat fat
200	2.8 g	1.5 g

Spinach and butternut squash bake

(V) | prep 20 minutes | cook 40 minutes | serves 2

for the baked vegetables
9 oz (250 g), peeled weight, butternut squash, seeded and cut into
    bite-size cubes
2 small red onions, peeled and each cut into 8 segments
2 tsp light vegetable or olive oil
freshly ground black pepper, to taste
4¼ oz (120 g) baby spinach leaves
1 tbsp water

for the white sauce
1 cup skim milk
scant ¼ cup cornstarch
1 tsp mustard powder
1 small onion, peeled
2 small bay leaves
4 tsp freshly grated vegetarian Parmesan or Pecorino cheese

for the topping
2 tbsp fresh whole-wheat bread crumbs

1. Preheat the oven to 400°F/200°C and warm an ovenproof serving dish.
2. Arrange the prepared squash and onions on a nonstick baking sheet and coat with the oil and plenty of pepper. Bake for 20 minutes, turning once.
3. To make the sauce, put the milk into a small nonstick pan with the cornstarch, mustard, onion, and bay leaves. Whisk over medium heat until thick. Remove from the heat, then discard the onion and bay leaves and stir in the cheese. Set aside, stirring occasionally, to prevent a skin forming.
4. When the squash is nearly cooked, put the spinach in a large pan with the water, stirring, for 2–3 minutes, or until just wilted.
5. You can continue cooking this dish in the hot oven, or preheat the broiler to medium-high. Put half the squash mixture in the warmed ovenproof dish and top with half the spinach. Repeat the layers. Pour over the white sauce and sprinkle over the bread crumbs.
6. Either put under the preheated broiler until browned and bubbling, or transfer to the oven for 15–20 minutes.

COOK'S TIP
• *Lightly boiled, steamed, or microwaved cauliflower florets can be added to the squash for extra bulk.*

NUTRITION INFORMATION
per serving

calories	fat	sat fat
120	3.9 g	1.4 g

Sweet and sour red cabbage

V | **prep** 5 minutes | **cook** 45–55 minutes | **serves** 2

7 oz (200 g) red cabbage, prepared weight, any tough core removed,
  finely sliced
1 medium cooking apple, peeled, cored, and chopped
1 shallot, peeled and finely chopped
1 tbsp wine vinegar, red or white
1 tbsp brown sugar
1 tsp butter
2 tbsp water
freshly ground black pepper, to taste

1. Put all the ingredients in a heavy-bottom, lidded pan or flameproof casserole.
Season to taste with pepper.
2. Cook over medium-low heat for 15 minutes, then stir well and replace the lid.
Reduce the heat and simmer for 30–40 minutes, stirring once or twice.
3. When the cabbage is tender, check the seasoning and serve.

COOK'S TIP
• *This dish can also be cooked in the oven, 325°F/160°C, for the
  same amount of time.*

NUTRITION INFORMATION

per serving

calories	fat	sat fat
105	2.5 g	1.4 g

Zucchini with mustard seeds

(V) | **prep** 5 minutes | **cook** 10–15 minutes | **serves** 2

1 tsp vegetable or
   olive oil
1 garlic clove, peeled and crushed
½ tsp black mustard seeds
½ tsp ground cumin
½ tsp coriander seeds
½ fresh red chili, seeded and
   finely chopped
2 medium zucchini, trimmed
   and sliced
7 oz (200 g) canned tomatoes,
   chopped
1 tbsp chopped fresh cilantro leaves
   or parsley

1. Heat the oil in a nonstick, lidded pan. Add the garlic, dry spices, and chili and stir over medium heat, then remove from the heat for 2 minutes.
2. Add the zucchini and tomatoes and cook for about 5–10 minutes, or until tender, adding 1 tablespoon of water if necessary. Stir in the cilantro and serve.

COOK'S TIP
• As a change from zucchini, try okra or serve the sauce over green beans.

Glazed parsnips with sesame seeds

(V) | **prep** 5 minutes | **cook** 20 minutes | **serves** 2

2 parsnips, peeled and cut into
   even-size chunks
1 tsp runny honey
½ tsp sesame seeds

1. Preheat the oven to 400°F/200°C.
2. Put the parsnips in a pan of water, bring to a boil, and cook for 5 minutes. Drain well.
3. Transfer the parsnips to a roasting pan and brush with the honey, then roast in the oven for 10 minutes.
4. Sprinkle over the sesame seeds and cook for an additional 5 minutes.

COOK'S TIP
• You can prepare carrots in the same way.

*Opposite fore-
ground: Glazed
parsnips with
sesame seeds;
background:
Zucchini with
mustard seeds*

NUTRITION INFORMATION

per serving

calories	fat	sat fat
60	2.5 g	0.5 g

NUTRITION INFORMATION

per serving

calories	fat	sat fat
100	2.0 g	0.4 g

173

Desserts

You don't have to miss out on dessert just because you're on a diet. Desserts don't have to be high in fat and sugar. Fresh fruit or a fruit salad is an excellent way to finish a meal and will help you reach the recommended target of 5 daily servings of fruit and/or vegetables. But if you fancy something a little more decadent, there are plenty of lowfat options available. Presentation plays an important role in our enjoyment of food and can transform a simple dessert into a special one. A sprig of fresh mint, a light dusting of confectioners' sugar, or a slice of fresh fruit as a garnish can make a real difference.

Meringues with lime cream and raspberries

🅥 | **prep** 5 minutes | **serves** 1

2½ tbsp plain yogurt (less than 2% fat)
2 tsp confectioners' sugar
grated zest and juice of ¼ lime
1 meringue nest
scant ¼ cup raspberries

1. Mix the yogurt, confectioners' sugar, and lime zest and juice together.
2. Place a meringue nest on a plate and pour in the yogurt mixture, then sprinkle with raspberries and serve.

COOK'S TIP
• *You can substitute frozen fruits of the forest for the raspberries or use fresh fruit in season.*

NUTRITION INFORMATION

per serving

calories	fat	sat fat
135	0.5 g	0.3 g

Strawberry and orange delight

prep 10 minutes + 30 minutes cooling | **cook** 5 minutes | **serves** 2

1¾ cups orange juice (see COOK'S TIP)
1 tbsp gelatin, or vegetarian equivalent (gelozone)
3¼ oz (90 g) small strawberries, sliced

1. Put scant ½ cup of the juice in a small heatproof bowl, then sprinkle over the gelatin and let stand for 5 minutes. Place the bowl over a pan of simmering water and stir until the gelatin melts and the liquid becomes clear, then stir in the remaining juice.
2. Divide the strawberries between 2 large wine glasses. Pour over enough juice to just cover the strawberries, then transfer to the refrigerator for 30 minutes, or until set.
3. Pour in the remaining juice and return to the refrigerator until set.

COOK'S TIPS
• *When strawberries are out of season, use seedless grapes instead.*
• *You could use another juice instead of orange, such as passion fruit (but not pineapple).*

NUTRITION INFORMATION

per serving

calories	fat	sat fat
130	0.2 g	trace

179

Spiced pineapple with mango sauce

V | **prep** 10 minutes | **cook** 5 minutes | **serves** 2

for the sauce
1 small ripe mango, peeled and pitted
½ cup orange juice
1 tsp arrowroot
½ tsp allspice
1 tsp melted butter
2 tsp raw sugar

2 thick slices fresh pineapple

1. First, make the sauce. Put the mango and orange juice in an electric blender and purée until smooth. Tip the purée into a small pan. Mix the arrowroot with a little cold water and add to the pan. Heat gently, stirring constantly, until the sauce begins to thicken.
2. Preheat the broiler to medium-high. Stir the allspice into the melted butter. Place the pineapple on a foil-covered baking sheet. Brush the pineapple with the melted butter, then sprinkle over the sugar and put under the broiler for 5 minutes.
3. Transfer the pineapple to a plate, then pour over a little of the sauce and serve warm (see COOK'S TIP).

COOK'S TIP
• *Decorate with delicate cape gooseberries for that added touch.*

NUTRITION INFORMATION
per serving

calories	fat	sat fat
145	2.4 g	1.4 g

Roasted peach with vanilla sugar

(V) | **prep** 10 minutes | **cook** 15–20 minutes | **serves** 1

for the vanilla sugar
¼ vanilla bean
scant 2 tbsp superfine sugar

1 small ripe peach, halved and pitted
2 tbsp lowfat plain yogurt

1. Preheat the oven to 400°F/200°C.
2. Scrape out the sticky seeds from the vanilla bean and blend with the sugar in an electric hand blender.
3. Place the peach, flesh-side up, in an ovenproof dish and sprinkle over the vanilla sugar.
4. Bake for 15–20 minutes, or until tender, and serve with plain yogurt.

COOK'S TIPS
• *If your peach is under-ripe, allow 20–30 minutes cooking time.*
• *This dish also works well with nectarines and plums—allow 1 nectarine or 2 plums per serving.*
• *A batch of vanilla sugar can be made ahead and kept for several weeks in a jar.*

NUTRITION INFORMATION
per serving

calories	fat	sat fat
140	0.2 g	0.2 g

183

Apple phyllo pockets with vanilla yogurt

(V) | prep 5 minutes | cook 20–25 minutes | serves 2

for phyllo pockets (makes 2)
1 medium tart cooking apple, peeled, cored, and cut into small chunks
2 tsp water
½ oz (15 g) golden raisins
2 tsp sugar
1 tsp lemon juice
pinch of ground cinnamon
6 sheets phyllo pastry, approximately ¾ x 1¼ inches (2 x 3 cm)
1 egg white, beaten
1 tbsp skim milk

for vanilla yogurt
few drops of vanilla extract
scant ½ cup lowfat plain yogurt, to serve

1. Preheat the oven to 400°F/200°C.
2. Put the apples in a small pan with the water. Simmer over gentle heat for a few minutes, or until the apples are just soft. Take care not to overcook the apples, as they will continue cooking in the oven.
3. Drain any excess liquid from the apples, then stir in the golden raisins, sugar, lemon juice, and cinnamon.
4. Take 3 sheets of phyllo, one on top of the other, and brush with the egg white. Spoon the apple mixture into the center and gather up the pastry edges to form a bag around the filling. Pinch the phyllo together with your fingers to seal it. Repeat with the remaining 3 sheets. Work quickly with the phyllo, as it goes dry quickly.
5. Place the pockets on a baking sheet and brush with the milk.
6. Bake for 20–25 minutes, or until golden brown. Let cool for a few minutes.
7. Stir the vanilla extract into the yogurt and serve with the phyllo pockets.

NUTRITION INFORMATION
per serving

calories	fat	sat fat
150	1.1 g	0.3 g

Baked banana with sin-free chocolate sauce

V | **prep** 1 minute | **cook** 10 minutes | **serves** 1

1 small banana
2 tsp corn syrup
3 tsp unsweetened cocoa

1. Preheat the oven to 350°F/180°C.
2. Bake the banana in its skin for 10 minutes, or until the skin is black.
3. Meanwhile, warm the syrup in a small pan over medium heat for 2–3 minutes, or in a medium-low microwave for 1 minute until very runny. Stir in the unsweetened cocoa until smooth and chocolate-like. Keep warm.
4. When the banana is cooked, discard the skin and put the flesh on a plate, then pour the chocolate sauce over and serve.

COOK'S TIP
• *You could, alternatively, bake your bananas on the grill until their skins turn black.*

NUTRITION INFORMATION
per serving

calories	fat	sat fat
140	2.6 g	0.6 g

Chocolate and orange liqueur mousse

prep 5 minutes + 40 minutes soaking | **serves** 1

Opposite left:
Chocolate and
orange liqueur
mousse; right:
Rum and raisin
chocolate mousse

½ tsp grated orange zest
1 tsp Cointreau
2½ oz (70 g) lowfat chocolate mousse
1 meringue nest, lightly crushed

1. Put the zest in an eggcup with the Cointreau and soak for at least 30 minutes.
2. Put the chocolate mousse in a bowl and stir in the meringue. Spoon into a sundae dish (see COOK'S TIP).
3. Refrigerate for at least 10 minutes, then serve with the orange zest and Cointreau spooned over.

COOK'S TIP

• *For an attractive layered effect (as shown opposite), spoon half the chocolate mousse into a sundae dish, followed by the meringue, followed by the rest of the mousse.*

Rum and raisin chocolate mousse

prep 10 minutes + 30 minutes soaking | **serves** 1

1 tsp raisins
1 tbsp dark rum
1 amaretto cookie, crumbled
   (optional)
2½ oz (70 g) lowfat chocolate mousse

1. Put the raisins in a teacup, then pour over the rum and let stand for at least 30 minutes, preferably overnight.
2. Stir the rum, raisins, and amaretto cookie into the chocolate mousse. Spoon into a sundae dish and serve.

COOK'S TIP

• *Amaretti cookies are a useful ingredient for slimming desserts because they are very light and are only 8% fat, but use them sparingly, as they are high in sugar.*

NUTRITION INFORMATION
per serving

calories	fat	sat fat
140	1.9 g	trace

NUTRITION INFORMATION
per serving

calories	fat	sat fat
150	2.3 g	1.2 g

Pear and chocolate cream

prep 5 minutes | can be made ahead and chilled | **serves** 1

2¾ oz (75 g), drained weight, canned pears in juice
generous ⅓ cup virtually fat-free ricotta
few drops of vanilla extract
½ square milk chocolate, grated

1. Purée the pears in an electric blender, or mash thoroughly with a fork.
2. In a mixing bowl, combine the pears, ricotta, and vanilla extract, then lightly stir in two-thirds of the chocolate.
3. Spoon into a single-serving dessert glass or dish and top with the remaining chocolate. Chill before serving.

NUTRITION INFORMATION
per serving

calories	fat	sat fat
150	4.7 g	2.7 g